1.1 John Snow, doctor and detective

This is about Doctor Snow's very clever use of maps over 160 years ago.

pages 6-7

1 Look at these statements. They describe what Doctor Snow did but are jumbled up. Write a number from 1-7 in the box to put them in the correct order.

- Work began on the sewage system in 1859
- Using a map of the area, Doctor Snow marked all the households where people had died
- On 31 August 1854, a cholera outbreak hit the area called Soho, in London
- Doctor Snow looked for patterns
- He also marked where the water pumps were.
- Within ten days, 500 were dead
- Doctor Snow thought that the water from the Broad Street pump was infected

2 Imagine it is 1857 and you are Doctor Snow. Write a letter to the government explaining why a new sewage system should be built. Try to be as persuasive as you can, and use facts and figures to support your ideas.

1.2 Meet GIS

geog.2
pages 8-9

This is about the exciting use of maps on a computer.

Imagine you are part of a group who are planning what should happen if a flood occurs in your town. You are working with a GIS expert to help develop your 'local' GIS map. The GIS expert suggests that you can choose six of the following layers on your GIS map:

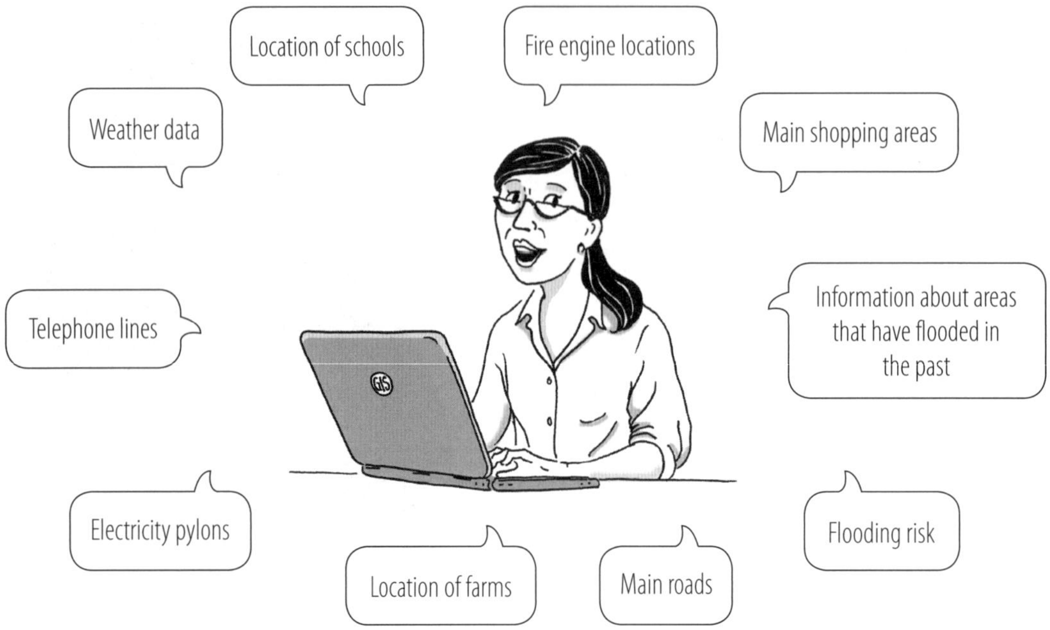

1 Colour in the six bubbles to show the layers of information that you would want on your GIS map.

2 Decide which you think is the most important information. Give reasons to explain your choice.

I think the most important information is ______________________________

____

____

3 Choose one of the layers that you decided was not needed on your map. Give reasons for your choice.

I did not include ______________ because ______________________

____

____

4 Can you think of one other piece of information that would be helpful to add as a layer to your GIS? In the space below state your layer and say why it would be useful.

____

____

Contents

1 Using GIS

You probably thought that a map was something that showed where places and other features in the world are found. With a GIS, however, maps can do so much more. There are three main types of map

- **Location maps** answer the question 'Where am I'?
- **Navigation maps** answer the question 'How do I get there'?
- **Spatial relationship (GIS) maps** are digital and help to answer the question – 'How are these things related or connected'?

1 For each of the following circle which of the above you would need to use.

This is my route to school (location / navigation / GIS)

I want to drive to Cornwall on holiday (location / navigation / GIS)

Where is Leeds? (location / navigation / GIS)

Can I grow crops here? (location / navigation / GIS)

This is where I live (location / navigation / GIS)

Where is the best place for our new recycling plant? (location / navigation / GIS)

Choose one of your answers and explain why you chose the answer you did.

2 GIS stands for Geographic Information System and there is a worldwide GIS Day that takes place in November each year. In the box below design an attractive postcard that would help advertise the day.

1.3 GIS in fighting crime

pages 10-11

All crimes have four aspects to them: a *law* is broken as an *offender* targets a *victim* at a particular *location*. GIS can help to solve crimes.

1 Write your own definition of an offender and a victim in the spaces below.

An offender is ____

____

A victim is ____

____

2 The map in the student book shows where crimes were committed. Look at the crimes recorded in grid square 1137. Write in the blog post below giving advice to people visiting the area. The blog post has been started for you.

> Tip: Be specific. Look at the types of crime and think about how people could avoid becoming crime victims.

Home **Blog Archive** **About**

Keeping safe

When visiting this area it is really important that you keep safe by...

3 You are in charge of controlling crime in the area. Where would you put most of your police resources? Name specific locations from the map and give reasons for your answer.

____

____

____

____

____

____

____

1.4 More about the data

The world is increasingly data rich. GIS helps us to effectively use data to solve problems.

pages 12-13

1 GIS needs data. Fill in the gaps in the following passage using words from the box beneath. Use the student book to help you.

The main purpose of GIS is to display __________ on a map, helping us to find __________, make __________ and decide on __________ to take. GIS data is very well-organised in __________. Each layer has one __________. A GIS allows us to turn layers on and off, so that we are only seeing the layers that are __________ to us.

theme decisions maps helpful actions layers data patterns

2 Look at these data layers for a new GIS investigation. People were asked in a survey if they would like to see a new shopping centre built.

Describe one investigation that this information would allow you to do. Explain how each of the data layers would help you.

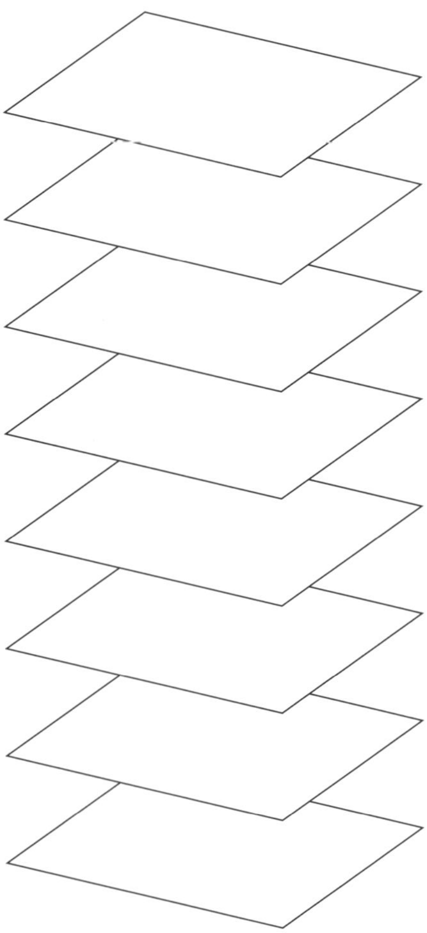

1.5 Other uses for GIS

The use of GIS affects our lives in many ways that we perhaps do not know!

geog.2 pages 14-15

1 Imagine you are a parcel! You are being sent on a journey from the Netherlands to Sheffield, in Yorkshire. Your route is shown below.

Scheduled Delivery:
Tuesday, 10/12/2013, By End of Day

Last Location:
Sheffield, United Kingdom, Tuesday, 10/12/2013

Change Delivery »

Request Status Updates »

▾ Additional Information

Shipped/Billed On:	06/12/2013
Type:	Package
Weight:	2.30 kgs

▾ Shipment Progress

Location	Date	Local Time	Activity
Sheffield, United Kingdom	10/12/2013	6:07	Out for Delivery
	10/12/2013	4:45	Arrival scan
Tamworth, United Kingdom	10/12/2013	3:21	Departure Scan
Tamworth, United Kingdom	09/12/2013	20:32	Arrival Scan
Barking, United Kingdom	09/12/2013	17:18	Departure Scan
	09/12/2013	12:33	Arrival Scan
Brussels, Belgium	09/12/2013	8:33	Departure Scan
Brussels, Belgium	07/12/2013	3:21	Arrival Scan
Eindhoven, Netherlands	06/12/2013	23:45	Departure Scan
	06/12/2013	20:26	Origin Scan
Netherlands	06/12/2013	14:07	Order Processed: Ready for UPS

7. Travel by van to customer

6. Travel by lorry to Sheffield airport

5. Travel by air to East Midland airport , then by van to Tamworth.

4. Travel by lorry to Barking, London

3. Travel by air to Heathrow airport, London

2. Travel by lorry to Brussels.

1. Travel by van to Eindhoven

In the space below, write a description of how GIS helped your journey.

Tip: Think about when your bar code would be scanned and who would be given that information – driver, parcel depot, customers.

2 Population

pages 16-17

1 Are these statements true or false? Put a tick in the correct box.

		True	**False**
a	We are not living as long as we used to do	☐	☐
b	Our numbers have been growing fast for 250 years	☐	☐
c	The population is falling in some countries	☐	☐
d	The world's population is unevenly spread	☐	☐
e	Our growing population has an impact upon the earth	☐	☐
f	The world's population is expected to reach 6 billion by 2025	☐	☐
g	5 000 new babies are born every single day	☐	☐

2 Distribution means the way in which something is shared out among a group or spread over an area. Write you own definition of population distribution in the space below. Compare your answer with a partner. Which of you has the most accurate definition?

____

____

____

3 Imagine the earth could write a letter to us. What do you think it would say about how it is expected to cope with the growing population?

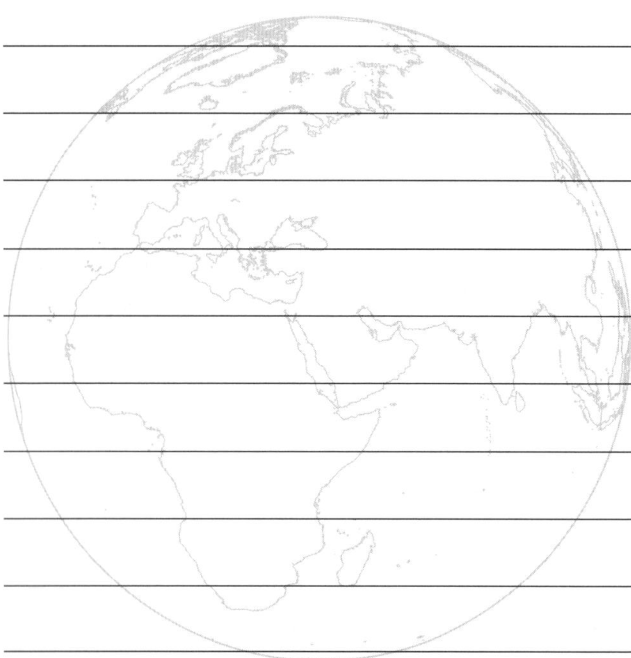

____

____

____

____

____

____

____

____

____

____

2.1 Our numbers are growing fast

This is about population change.

pages 18-19

1 Use arrows to link the key terms below to their correct definitions.

birth rate	birth rate minus death rate
natural increase	the number of deaths each year for every 1000 people
death rate	the number of births each year for every 1000 people

2 Draw a coffin shape next to those factors below which you think would increase the death rate. Draw a baby shape next to those factors which would increase the birth rate. Two have been done for you.

- dirty water 
- young age of marriage 
- reliable food supply
- lots of disease
- children begin working when young
- war
- no contraception
- not enough food

3 Write down two factors that you think would reduce the death rate. Explain why.

Factor	Explanation

4 Using the table below, calculate which countries have a rising population, and which a falling one. Take away the death rate from the birth rate. One has been done for you.

	Birth rate/1000	Death rate/1000	Natural increase/1000
Ghana	42	33	9
Italy	7	9	
UK	9	10	
Mexico	21	11	
India	30	18	

2.2 So where is everyone?

This is about countries with lots of people, and places with hardly any.

pages 20-21

1 We call countries with lots of people densely populated, and countries with few people s _ _ _ _ _ _ _ populated.

2 Look at the map. You will notice that Greenland and India have been left blank. Use the key to shade in the country that you think is densely populated, and leave the other country blank.

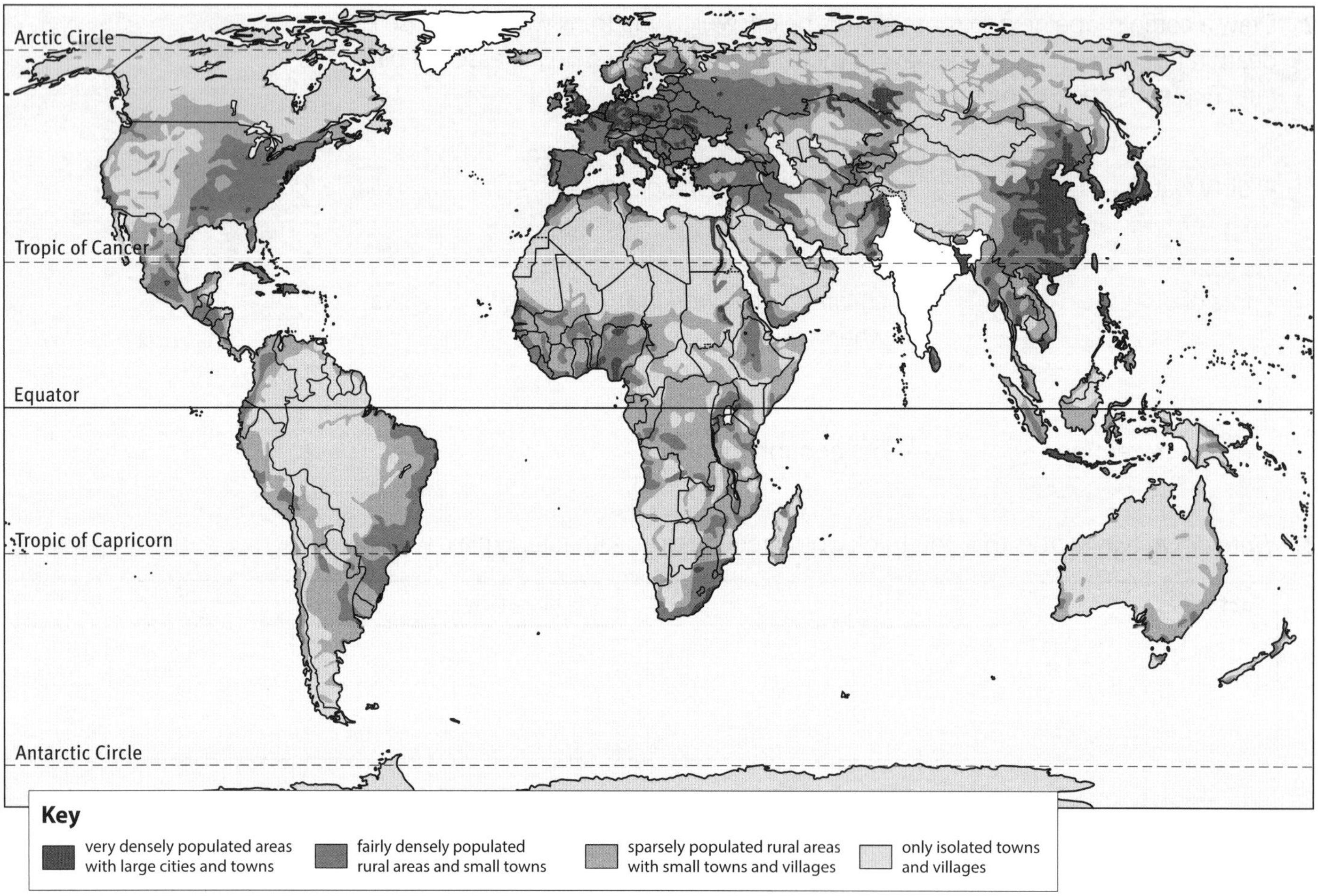

3 Look at the map again, and decide which of the following statements are true and which are false. Put T or F in the box beside each statement.

a The northern hemisphere is more crowded than the southern hemisphere. ☐

b Places near the poles are more densely populated than places near the tropics. ☐

c Africa is more densely populated than Europe. ☐

d Australia is more sparsely populated than Japan. ☐

e The population of South America is evenly distributed across the continent. ☐

2.3 The population of the UK

This is about how the UK's population has changed over time.

pages 22-23

> Tip: Remember that there may be both good and bad points – try to think of both.

1 The Industrial Revolution saw the setting up of many factories. Imagine you are one of the child workers shown in the photograph in the student book. Write forty words describing how you feel about your work.

____

____

____

____

____

2 Since 1801 the government has held a census or population count every 10 years. Before this it had no idea how many people lived in the UK. What problems do you think this may have caused for the government?

____

____

____

3 More of the UK population is living longer. This will bring with it some challenges for the country. These may be economic (to do with money) or social (to do with people). Think of two challenges and write your answers in the space below. An example of one of each has been done to help you.

Challenges	
Economic	Social
More money needed for pensions may make the country poorer.	More elderly people may be living on their own.

4 Imagine you are the Prime Minister. For one of the answers above, write down what you would do to help meet the challenge.

____

____

Population around the world

pages 24-25

This is about population growth and life expectancy around the world.

1 Draw lines to match the heads and tails of these sentences.

Population is rising fastest in Africa…

The earth's human population is growing at about 1.2% each year…

Population growth is generally faster…

…which is the poorest continent

…the northern hemisphere

The countries where the population is falling are found in…

…which adds over 80 million people to earth each year

…in poorer less-developed countries

2 Population is growing fastest in some of the world's poorest countries. Choosing the correct words from the box, complete the paragraph below to explain why.

In poorer countries most people live by ____________. Children are a form of ____________, as they will help on the farm and look after their parents as they become ____________. Many women do not have access to ____________ about family life, and so many have babies one after another. Many girls have little ____________ as they leave primary school early and are very poorly ____________. They may be ____________ very young and they may have little say in how many children they have. Their ____________ are in control.

advice	educated	married	security	choice	old	farming	husbands

3 Low life expectancy is the result of poverty, lack of access to clean water, food and medical help. Look at the items shown in the Aid Bag below. Colour in the one that you think would be most helpful in raising life expectancy. Explain the reasons for your choice.

Water tank

Appointment with doctor

Farming advice

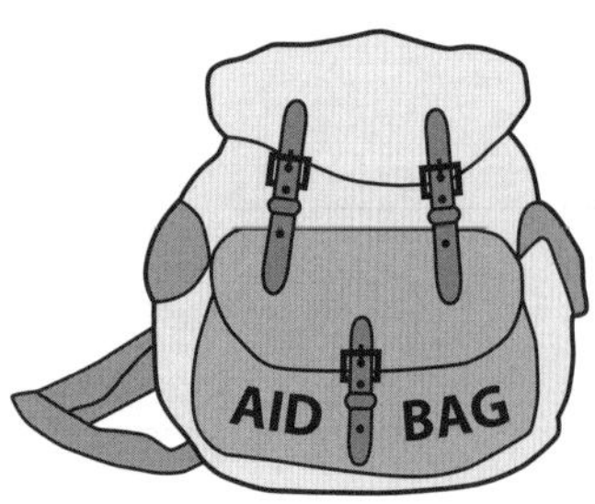

Water purification tablets

£1000

Free schooling

____

____

____

2.5 Our impact on our planet

pages 26-27

This is about our increasing use of resources and what the future may be like as a result.

1 Using the information from the student book, complete the spider diagram to show how the demand for the world's resources is growing. One has been done for you.

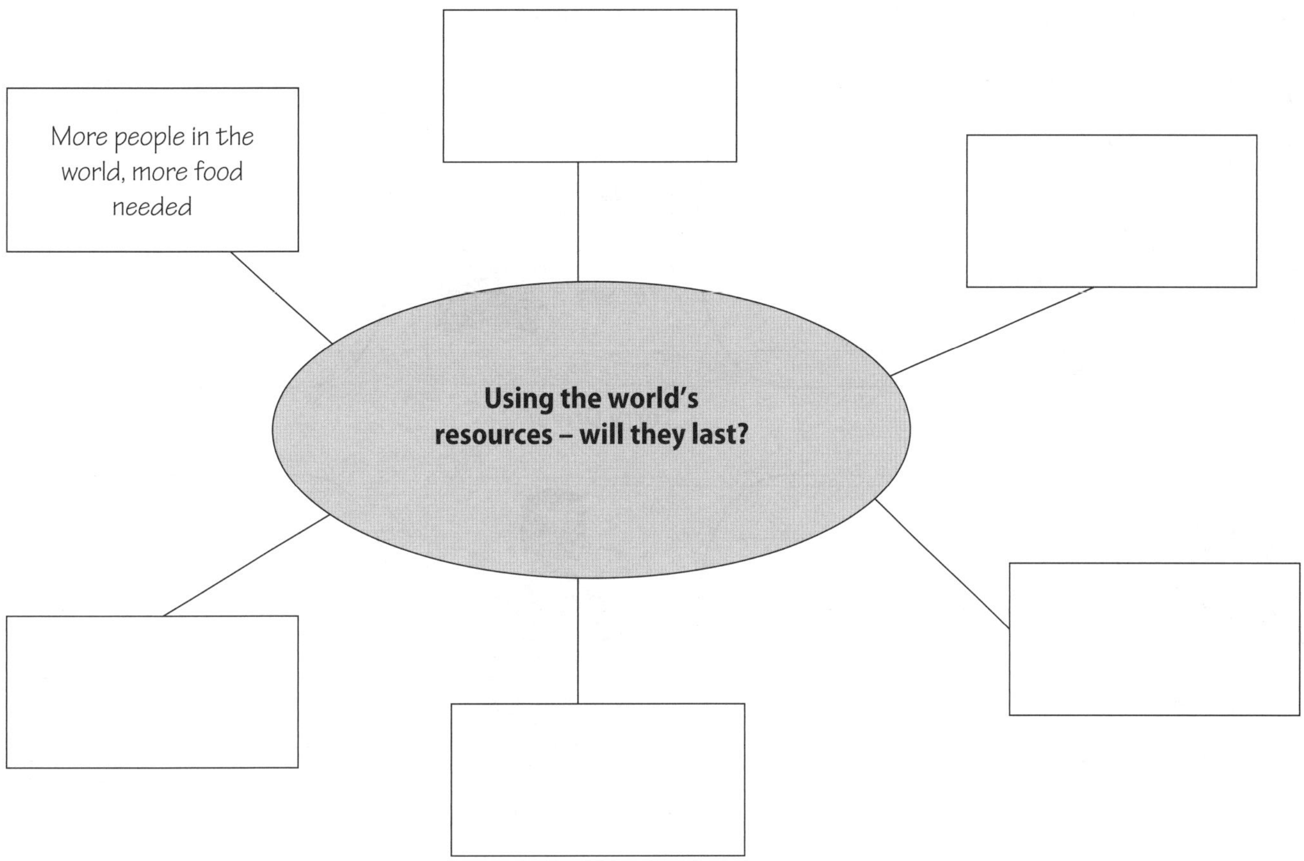

2 We can all help the planet by living in a more sustainable way. Here are some examples.

A Walk, don't drive

B Recycle and re-use

C Don't use plastic bags

D Buy locally grown food

Choose one of the above and explain why you think it would help our planet.

Example chosen: ______________________________

Explanation: ______________________________

____

____

____

____

2.6 What does the future hold?

pages 28-29

This is about using evidence to plan for a growth in population.

1 The UK's population may reach 77 million by the year 2050 – that is an extra 13 million people living in the UK compared to today. How do you think this may affect our lives? Add words to the speech bubbles below to explain the effects of this population growth on each of the people and their jobs.

Hospital Doctor

Lorry Driver

Teacher

National Park warden

2 The United Nations has chosen 11 July as World Population Day, to help raise awareness of the challenges and opportunities that a rising world population will bring. The Secretary-General, Ban Ki-moon, gave this message for World Population Day on 11 July 2014.

"On this World Population Day, I call on all with influence to prioritise youth in development plans, strengthen partnerships with youth-led organisations, and involve young people in all decisions that affect them. By empowering today's youth, we will lay the groundwork for a more sustainable future for generations to come"

Do you think that young people can provide the answer to halting the growth in world population? Give reasons for your answer.

3 Urbanisation

pages 30-31

1 You may live in an urban area or you may have visited a nearby town or city. Circle the two words from those shown below that best describe what you think about this place. For each, give reasons for your choice.

scary | lively | developed | entertaining | dirty | dangerous

happy | fun | built-up | noisy | deprived | diverse

I have chosen ____________ because ____

____

I have chosen ____________ because ____

____

2 Imagine that you live in the urban area shown in the photo on page 30 in the student book. You have been tweeted by a friend asking you to convince them why it would be good to move to live there. Write your reply - remember just 140 characters long, including spaces!

Tip: Be as persuasive as you can in your writing! **!**

____

____

____

____

3 In the space below draw a picture that shows either the advantages or disadvantages of living in an urban area.

Advantages / Disadvantages (circle one)

3.1 How our towns and cities grew

pages 32-33

This is an exercise about the reasons behind the growth in world urbanisation.

1 A list of reasons behind the growth of urbanisation is shown below, but they are in the wrong order. Put the list in the correct order, by writing a number from 1 to 7 in the correct box.

The Industrial Revolution meant factories were built near towns so they could get workers

Some villages grew into market towns

Towns became bigger and bigger, and some became cities

Clusters of dwellings became settlements

New farm machinery, built in factories, meant that not so many farm workers were needed

Villages grew around markets

Farm workers moved to towns to find work in factories

2 What are the consequences of a growth in urbanisation? Write your answers into the hexagons below. Two examples have been done for you. Try to give a balance of ideas – the consequences do not all need to be negative!

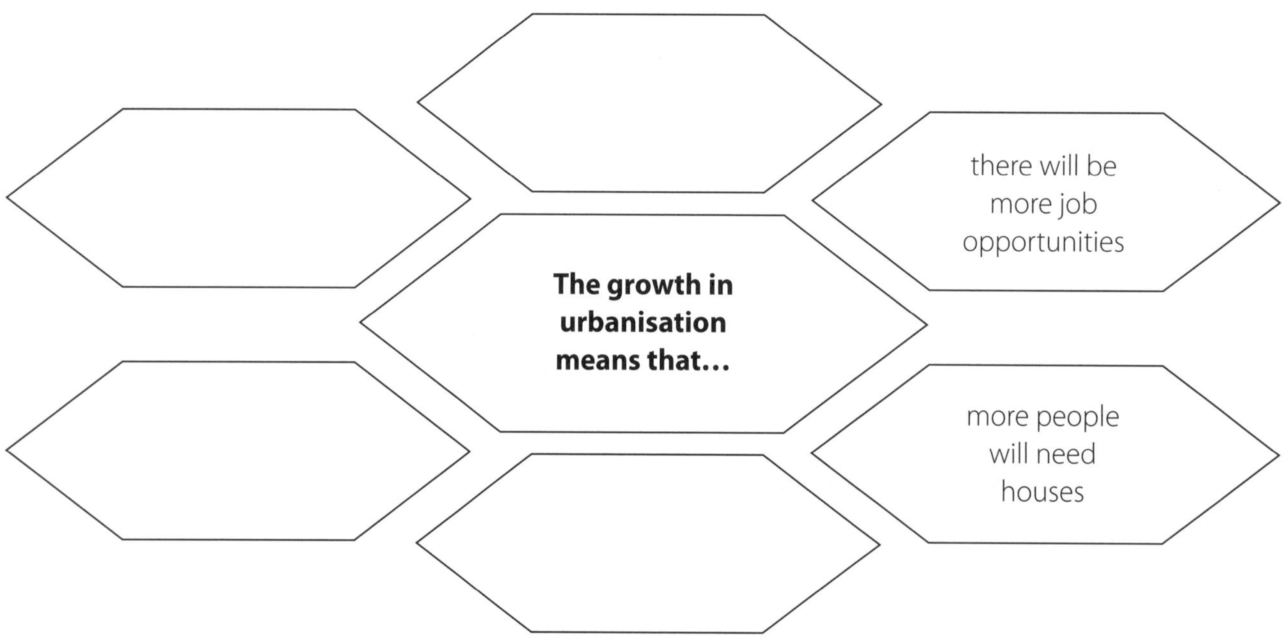

3 Now try to make links between the outer hexagons. For example, more job opportunities will mean that people may be able to afford to rent or buy housing. Compare your answers with a partner.

3.2 Manchester's story – part 1

geog.2 pages 34-35

This is about the early urbanisation of the city of Manchester.

1 Study the photograph below. In the spaces around the photo write down one thing that you do know about the photograph, two things that you don't know and three things that you would like to know more about.

I know …

I dont know …

I dont know …

I would like to know …

I would like to know …

I would like to know …

2 Imagine you lived in Manchester at this time, and you worked in a mill. Write about what you think your typical working day would be like? You must use the words below in your answer.

tired	safety	painful	poor

____

____

____

____

____

____

____

3.3 Manchester's story – part 2

This is about Manchester's more recent population changes.

pages 36-37

1 Look at the graph on page 36 in the student book. Circle the letter to show in which section of the graph – a to f – each of these statements would likely to have happened. Explain why you chose your section of the graph rather than another one.

Some shops close as the population falls   a   b   c   d   e   f

Reason ____

____

Hospitals are overcrowded   a   b   c   d   e   f

Reason ____

____

Thousands of new houses are built   a   b   c   d   e   f

Reason ____

____

Welcome to MediaCityUK, a new waterfront destination for Greater Manchester, with digital creativity, learning and leisure at its heart.

The BBC and ITV both operate at MediaCityUK, producing thousands of hours of content for television, radio and online.

Salford University also operates at MediaCityUK and says "it is a vibrant place in which to live, work, socialise and study."

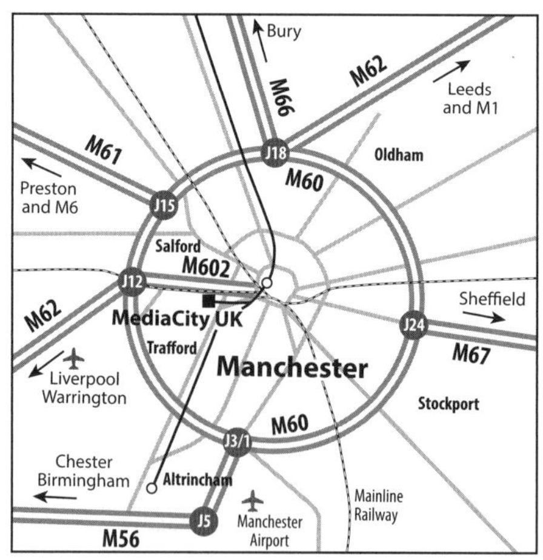

2 MediaCityUK has been developed on the Manchester Ship Canal, on the site of the docks where much of Manchester's trade was carried out. It has been said that it represents Manchester's future. How far do you agree with this statement? Give reasons for your answer below.

____

____

____

____

3.4 Urbanisation around the world

This is your chance to find out about urbanisation in other countries around the world.

pages 38-39

Over the last ten years, the number of people living in megacities with over 10 million people has increased tenfold. According to the 2011 United Nations report on world population prospects, this trend will only increase, with one out of every five people on earth expected to live in a megacity by 2025.

Rank	City	2011 population	Projected Annual Growth Rate	Estimated Population in 2025	Potential Natural Hazard
1	Lagos, Nigeria	11.2 million	3.71%	18.9 million	None
2	Dhaka, Bangladesh	15.4 million	2.84%	22.9 million	Cyclone Drought Flooding
3	Shenzhen, China	10.6 million	2.71%	15.5 million	Cyclone Drought Flooding
4	Karachi, Pakistan	13.9 million	2.68%	20.2 million	Cyclone Drought Flooding
5	Delhi, India	22.7 million	2.67%	32.9 million	Drought Flooding

1 The United Nations report that most of these cities are also at risk from natural hazards. Use an atlas to locate the five cities in the table above on the world map below. The, write a letter to the United Nations explaining why the expected population growth in these cities may cause problems.

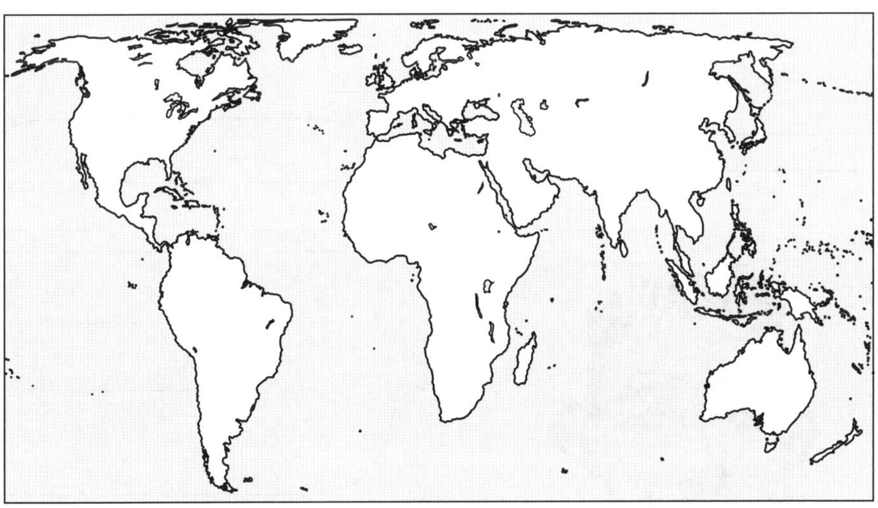

Tip: Think about the impacts on the environment, on people and on the economy of the country and city.

3.5 Why do people move to urban areas?

This is where you will discover the reasons why people move from the countryside to cities.

pages 40-41

1 Think about your own life. Write down three reasons why you might choose to move to another town, city or country in the future. Explain, for each, whether it would be caused by a push or pull factor.

	Reason for moving	Push / Pull	Explanation
1			
2			
3			

2 For each of your own reasons above, describe one change to your own area that would mean that you would not be tempted to move.

3.6 It's not all sunshine!

This is where you will discover whether you would be suited to city life.

pages 42-43

1 Page 42 of the student book shows some of the benefits and disadvantages of city life. Choose any three of each and list them below.

Benefits of city life	Disadvantages of city life

2 In the space below design an area of a city where you would like to live. It should have each of your chosen benefits, but also should have some design features that mean the disadvantages are no longer a problem!

Tip: Think as creatively as you can and give your city an appropriate name!

3.7 Life in the slums

This is where you will find out about the poorest people who live in cities.

pages 44-45

1 The paragraph below describes life in the slums.

Circle the correct word from each pair. Use page 44 in the student book to help you.

Cities are growing **fast / slow** in developing countries. Many slums are made from anything the people can find, and have **no / some** running water. Around **half / one-third** of people in developing countries live in slums. That is **860 / 86** million people in all. Osakwe lives in a slum in **Lisbon / Lagos**. Nine people live in **two / four** rooms, so it is very crowded. There is a lot of rubbish, and people throw it into the **ditch / bins** outside the house.

2 Look at the photographs of the slums in the student book. Choose three adjectives to describe what they are like. One adjective should have 4 letters, one should have 6 with the last having 8 letters.

Adjective 1 (4 letters) __________ **Adjective 2** (6 letters) ____________________

Adjective 3 (8 letters) ______________________________

3 One way to tackle the slum problem is through self-help schemes, and many British charities support these. Save the Children, a British charity, set up in 1919, also say that:

'Education is many children's route out of poverty. It gives them a chance to gain valuable knowledge and skills, and to improve their lives. And it means when they grow up, their children will have a much better chance of surviving and thriving.'

If you were making the decision on how to spend £5 million to help people like Osakwe in the slums of Lagos, would you spend it on schools and teachers, or building materials for houses? You have a difficult choice.
Write a letter to the Nigerian government explaining your decision.

3.8 A city of the future?

This is where you can display your creativity!

pages 46-47

1 Masdar City aims to be the world's most sustainable city. The Abu Dhabi royal family want the world to know about it and have asked you to create an eye-catching poster to tell the world. The six aims are shown below but you have also been asked to think of two other aims that you think should form part of this exciting project. Draw pictures in the spaces below to create your poster, and don't forget to add your own special sustainable aims at the end!

Avoid fossil fuels	Keep cool
Be walkable	Allow high population density
Have car-free streets	Minimise waste
______________________	______________________

4 Coasts

1 What does a coast mean to you? In the space below draw a picture of a coastal scene. If you live on the coast, it could be where you live. Or perhaps a scene you remember from a holiday? Or it could be an imaginary coast anywhere in the world. Add labels or text to your drawing if you want to.

2 Write down two things you know about coasts.

a ______________________________

b ______________________________

3 Write down two things you would like to know about coasts.

a ______________________________

b ______________________________

4 At the end of this topic, come back and see if you've found out about these things If you have, draw a ☺ next to your question - if you haven't, draw a ☹!

4.1 Waves and tides

This is about what causes the waves and tides, and the different types of waves.

geog.2

pages 50-51

1 Choose words from the box to fill in the gaps in the sentences below.

sun	weak	boats	wind	moon	big	small	long
backwash	short	fetch	carry	strong	swash		

Waves are made by ________________ pulling on the surface of the water.

The length of water over which the wind blows is called the ________________ .

Large waves are made by:

✓ ________________ wind

✓ the wind blowing for a ________________ time

✓ a ________________ fetch

The water that goes up the beach when a wave breaks is called the ________________ .

The water that goes back down the beach is called the ________________ .

Tides are caused by the pull of the ________________ .

2 Write the correct caption from the bullet list below underneath each diagram of a wave.

- If a wave is high and steep, it erodes the beach.
- If a wave is high and steep, it builds up the beach.
- If a wave is low and flat, it erodes the beach.
- If a wave is low and flat, it builds up the beach.

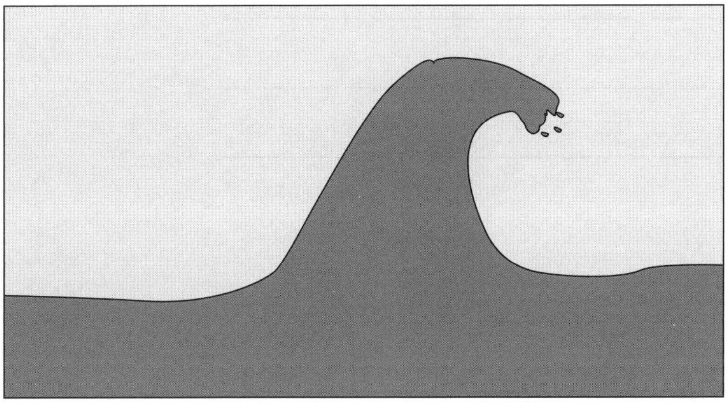

____

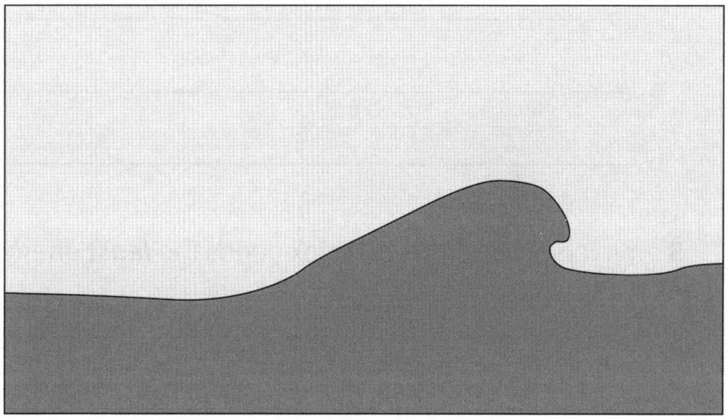

____

4.2 The waves at work

This is about what jobs waves do.

pages 52-53

1 Write these phrases into the correct part of the table below.

- the process is called longshore drift
- how the waves wear away the coast
- a beach is made like this
- when waves drop the load they are carrying
- low flat waves drop material
- material is moved in a zig-zag by the swash and the backwash
- the four processes are called solution, hydraulic action, attrition and abrasion
- when material is carried along the coast

erosion	transport	deposition

2 Which process do you think needs the ***most*** energy? Why?

____

____

____

____

3 Which process do you think needs the ***least*** energy? Why?

____

____

____

____

4.3 Landforms created by the waves

This is about how coastal landforms are made.

pages 54-55

1 The diagram below shows several coastal landforms. Add the labels from the box to it.

crack
cave
stack
wave-cut platform

2 Explain how waves have created the landforms in the diagram.

____

____

____

____

3 What do you think will happen to these landforms next? Why?

____

____

____

____

Draw a diagram of your prediction here:

4.4 The coast and us

This is about how the coast is used in many ways by different groups of people.

geog.2
pages 56-57

Natural
This is about the environment – energy, air, water, soil, living things.

Who decides
This is about who makes choices and decides what is to happen.

Economic
This is about money, trade, buying and selling.

Social
This is about people and the way they live their lives.

To help you remember these four points, think; **N**orth, **E**ast, **S**outh, **W**est.

1 Look carefully at the photo above and the four 'points of the compass' around it.

Write down how people may affect the coastline in natural, economic and social ways.

Natural ______________________________

Economic ______________________________

Social ______________________________

2 Choose one of your three answers.

Write in more detail about how people may have good or bad effects on the coast.

Natural / Economic / Social (circle your choice)

____

____

____

____

4.5 Your holiday in Newquay

This is about using an OS map to find out more about Newquay.

pages 58-59

1 In the spaces below, fill in details for an information leaflet for tourists who want to visit Newquay. Look at the OS map on page 23 of the pupil book to help you.

Newquay in Cornwall

A holiday for all ages!

Beaches

____

____

____

Countryside

____

____

____

Things to do

____

____

____

2 You could travel to Newquay by road, rail or air.
Choose how you would travel to Newquay and explain why.
Is your chosen method sustainable?

I would travel to Newquay by road / rail / air (circle your choice)
I would travel this way because

____

____

____

____

4.6 Under threat from the sea

The floods of the winter of 2013-2014 had a major impact on the country. Can you remember what happened?

pages 60-61

Were you or where you live affected by the floods during the winter of 2013/2014? If so, write an account of what happened to you or to other people where you live. If you were not directly affected, write an account of what you saw on the TV, heard about through social media or read in the newspapers. You will find plenty of information to remind you on the internet.

____

____

____

____

____

____

____

____

____

____

____

4.7 How long can Happisburgh hang on?

This is about how one village is falling into the sea!

pages 62-63

1 The boxes on the right explain why the village is falling into the sea. But they are in the wrong order! Write the correct order in the circles.

2 This diagram shows what is happening. Label:

groynes revetments cliff houses at risk beach

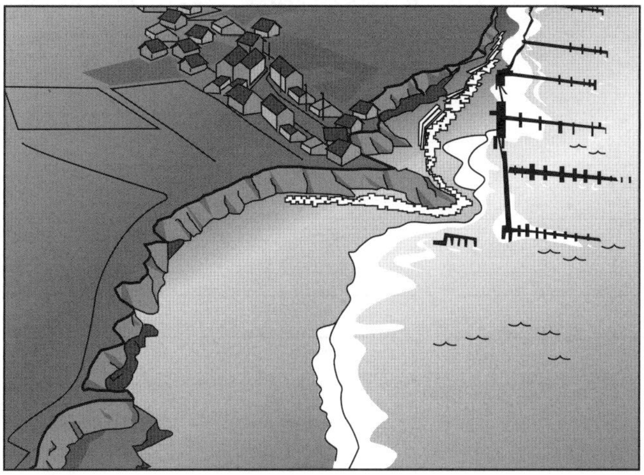

- The clay slides out of the bottom of the cliff and the sand on top collapses. ◯
- All the time, the sea is also taking chunks out of the bottom of the cliffs by wave erosion. ◯
- The cliffs are sand on top of clay below. ◯
- The clay gets wet and the water makes it slippery. ◯
- Rain can get through the sand to the clay. ◯

3 The people whose homes are destroyed can't get the money from insurance. Cliff falls are called 'Acts of God' and aren't covered by insurance.

a How do you think the people feel about this? Why?

____

____

____

____

b Do you think they should get compensation? Why / why not? (Think about everyone else's insurance premiums, the amount taxes might go up, whether it's fair …)

____

____

____

____

4.8 Protecting places from the sea

This is about how planners are trying to prevent erosion at the coast.

geog.2 pages 64-65

1 The pictures below show ways to reduce erosion.

a For each one, write a title at the top. Choose from:
Sea wall, Wave-break, Beach replenishment, Groynes, Pipes, Rock armour.

1 ______

2 ______

3 ______

4 ______

5 ______

6 ______

b Underneath each picture explain how the method works.

c Which method do you think is most effective? Why?

d Which one do you think is least effective? Why?

5 Weather and climate

pages 66-67

1 What is the climate like where you live?

What are the good things about it and what are the bad things?

Good things	**Bad things**
____________________	____________________
____________________	____________________
____________________	____________________
____________________	____________________
____________________	____________________
____________________	____________________

2 How do you rate your climate?

Rate your climate for the following factors on a scale of 1 to 10. (1 means you think there's too little of it, 10 means you think there's too much). Then compare your decisions with those of your friends. Discuss the reasons for your ratings.

Rain

1	2	3	4	5	6	7	8	9	10
☐	☐	☐	☐	☐	☐	☐	☐	☐	☐

Sun

1	2	3	4	5	6	7	8	9	10
☐	☐	☐	☐	☐	☐	☐	☐	☐	☐

Wind

1	2	3	4	5	6	7	8	9	10
☐	☐	☐	☐	☐	☐	☐	☐	☐	☐

3 Imagine if the climate was the same all over the world. What impact would this have on the way we all live?

____

____

____

____

5.1 It's the weather!

This is about how the weather affects different people and you!

pages 68-69

1 Add words to the speech bubbles to explain how different types of weather could affect the following people.

Lorry driver

Farmer

Hotel owner

Supermarket manager

2 Think about how the weather affects you. Sometimes it is fun, and sometimes it is not! Write about one way that the weather has affected you.

Type of weather ______________________________

5.2 So what causes weather?

This is about the main causes of weather.

pages 70-71

1 Look at the picture below which shows the two main ways that weather can be caused.
A Key Stage 2 teacher has asked you to write an explanation for her class of nine year olds.
Write your explanations in the boxes below using page 70 of the pupil book to help you.
Add pictures if it would help them to understand!

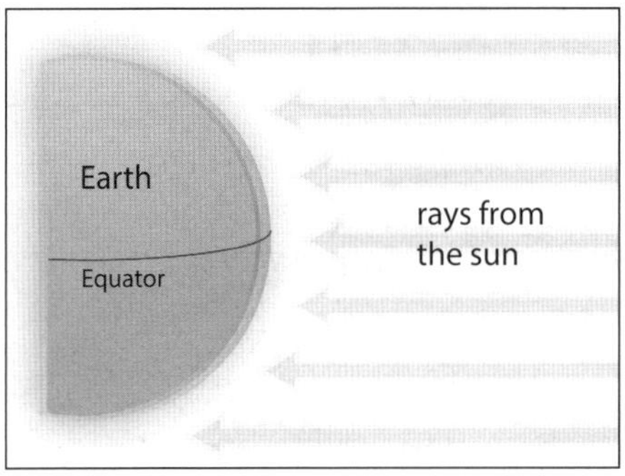

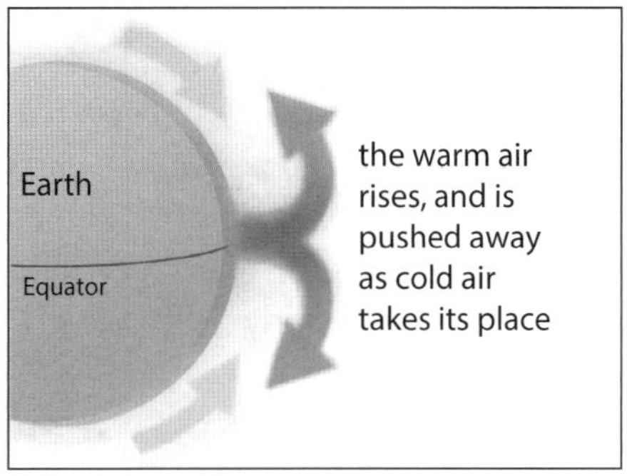

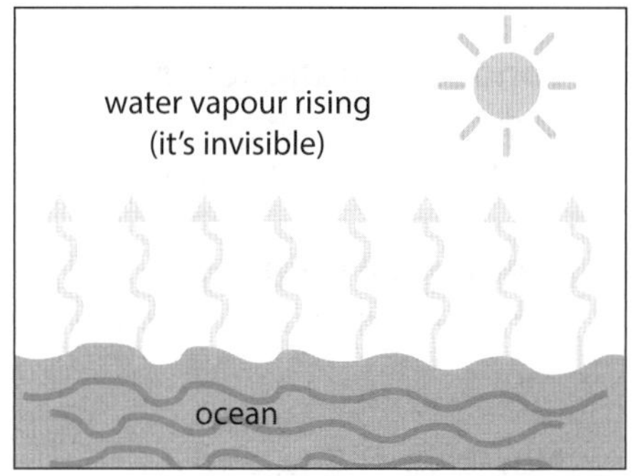

2 Fill in the gaps in this paragraph about water vapour. Choose words from this list

evaporate grass hang condense gas dew

Water vapour is a ____________ . In cold weather it may ____________ around us as fog, or it may ____________ in the air as mist. Sometimes it condenses on cold ____________ and leaves and becomes ____________ .
When the sun shines, all of these ____________ again.

5.3 Measuring the weather

This is about mapping the weather, and how it is measured.

pages 72-73

1 What is weather? Write your definition here.

____

2 Read the weather descriptions below for four areas of the UK. Then look at the weather symbols box. Draw the correct weather symbols in the boxes on the map to match the description of the weather in that area.

London and the south east
Mainly dry and bright with spells of sunshine, but also risk of showers. Maximum 9 °C. 5 mph south-westerly winds.

South west England
Long periods of heavy rain. Maximum 8 °C. 10 mph westerly winds.

North west England
Cloudy with risk of showers. Maximum 7 °C. 5 mph westerly winds.

North east Scotland
Dry and bright. Maximum 8 °C. 10 mph south-westerly winds.

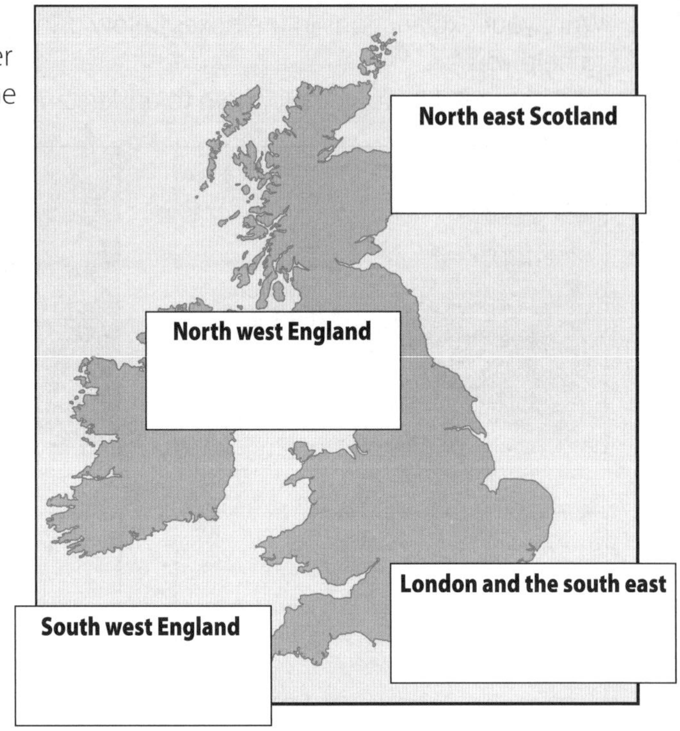

(The figure in the circle is the wind speed. The arrow shows the direction of the wind.)

16 (Use numbers for temperature.)

3 Put a ring round the odd one out in each set below. Explain your choice of odd one out.

a °C millibars wind speed oktas

Explanation: ____

b temperature thermometer precipitation cloud cover

Explanation: ____

c anemometer barometer rain gauge km/h

Explanation: ____

d sun snow drizzle rain

Explanation: ____

5.4 More about rain … and clouds

This is about three types of rainfall.

geog.2 pages 74-75

1 These pictures show three different types of rainfall. Write the text beside each picture in the correct box on the picture.

Convectional rainfall

The rising air cools. The water vapour condenses. Clouds form. It rains.

The sun warms the ground … which then warms the air above it.

Currents of warm air rise.

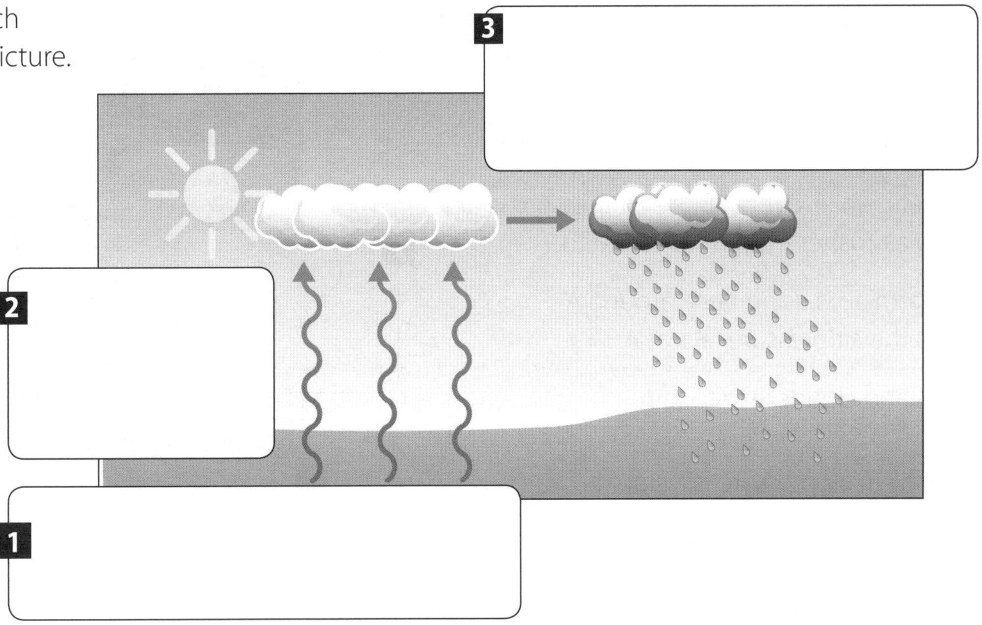

Relief rainfall

The rising air cools. The water vapour condenses. Clouds form. It rains.

Warm moist air arrives from the Atlantic Ocean.

The rain falls on the windward side of the mountain. The leeward side stays dry.

The air is forced to rise.

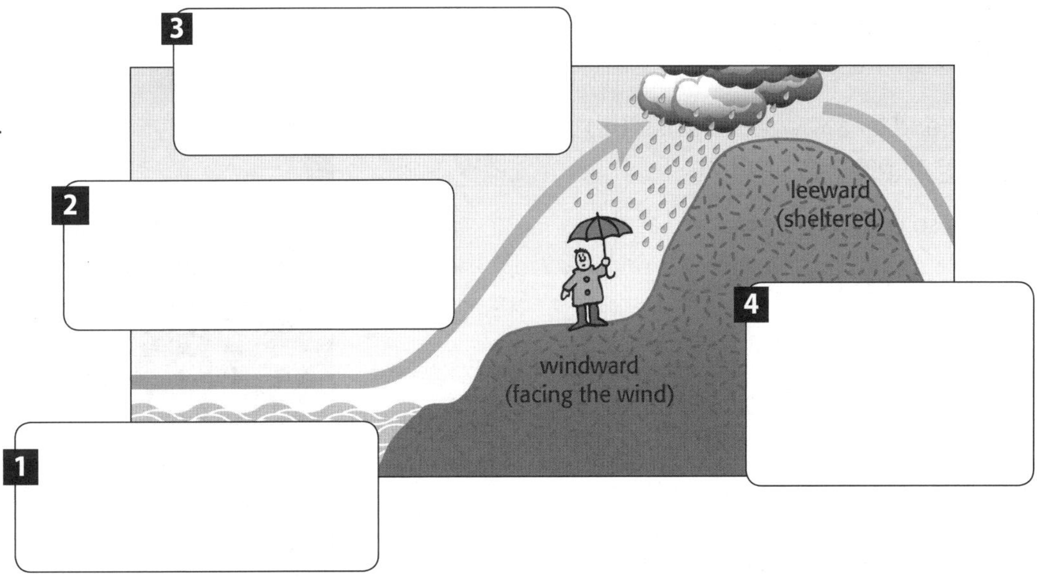

Frontal rainfall

The warm air mass slides up over the cold one, or gets driven up by it.

A warm air mass meets a cold air mass.

The rising air cools. The water vapour condenses. Clouds form. It rains.

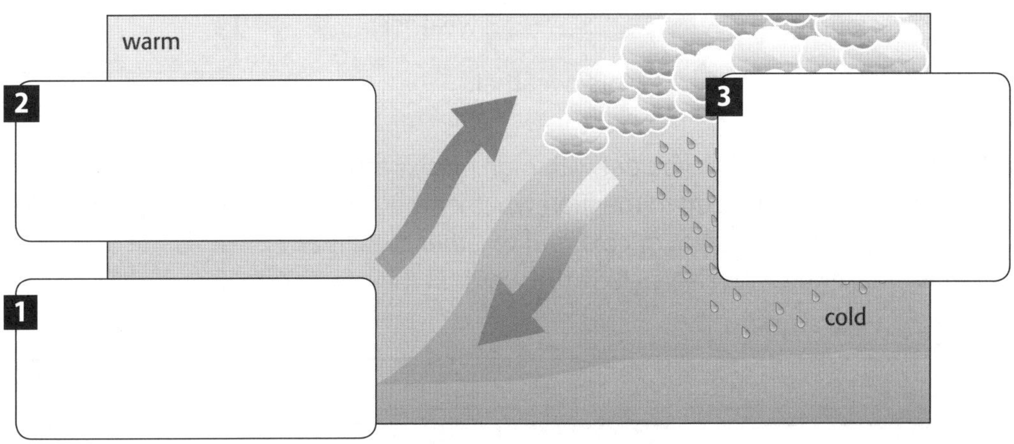

5.5 Air pressure

This is about the weather you get with high and low air pressure.

pages 76-77

1 The pictures show low and high pressure weather. Write the text below in the correct box on each picture, then complete the sentences underneath.

But warm rising air means clouds form …

Meanwhile, over at B the air pressure is higher. So air rushes from B to A as wind.

Warm air is rising here, around A. So the air pressure falls at A.

… and clouds lead to rain.

Low pressure weather

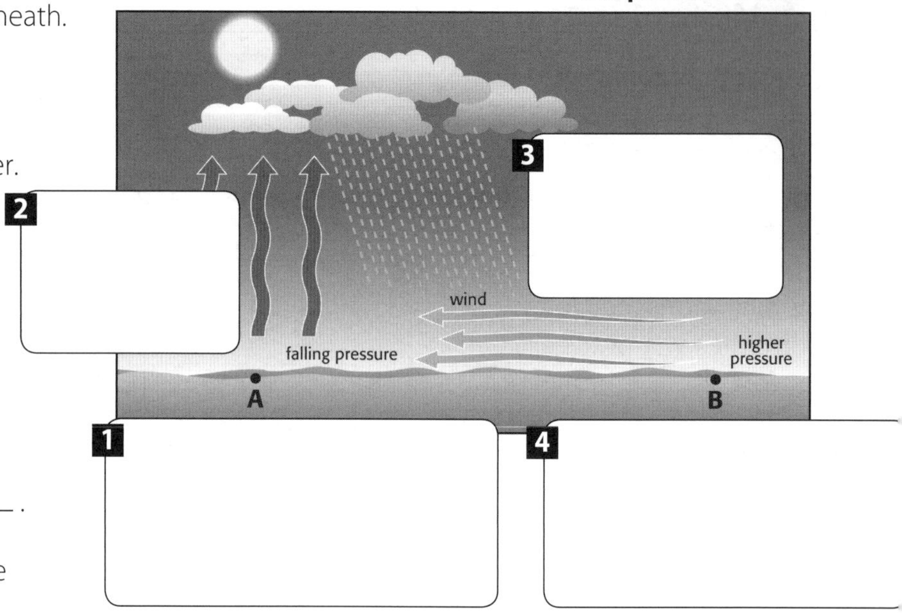

A fall in air pressure is a sign of

________________ and ________________ .

The lower the ________________ the worse

the ________________ will be.

… and far away, at Y, it sinks. This causes the air pressure at Y to rise.

… so cold air gets pushed aside …

Now Y has high pressure.

Warm air is rising at X …

As the cold air sinks it warms up. So no water vapour condenses and no clouds form over Y. The sky stays clear.

High pressure weather

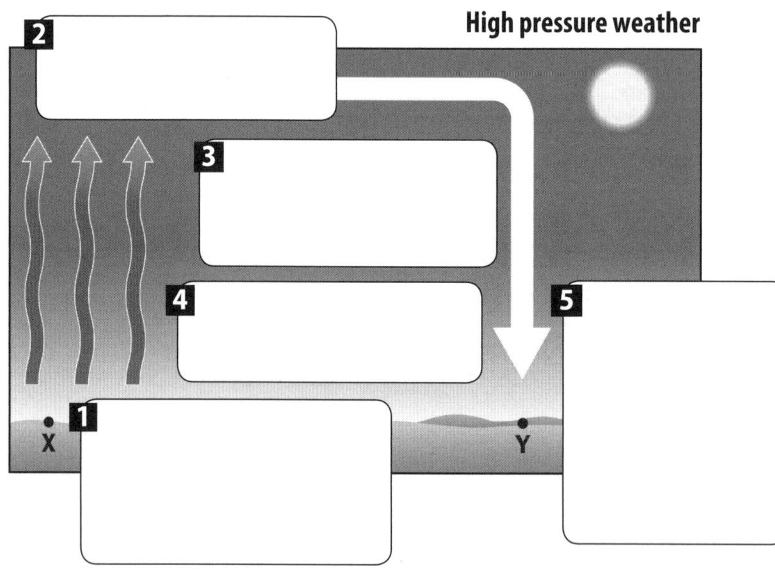

High pressure means no ________________.

It gives our hottest ________________ weather

and ________________ winter weather.

2 Describe the weather you get with high pressure in winter and summer. You need to mention whether there are any clouds, whether it is hot or cold, and whether there is any rain. Make sure you also include the words in the box.

frost dew thunderstorms fog drought flooding

____

____

5.6 Why is our weather so changeable?

This is about why our weather in the UK changes so quickly.

pages 78-79

1 Are these statements true or false? Put a tick in the correct box.

		True	False
a	The air moves around the world in huge blocks called air masses.	☐	☐
b	A warm air mass brings strong gusty wind and heavy rain.	☐	☐
c	An air mass coming from the North Pole will be warm and damp.	☐	☐
d	The leading edge of an air mass is called a front.	☐	☐
e	A cold air mass brings wind and rain.	☐	☐
f	When a new air mass reaches the UK, it brings a change in the weather.	☐	☐
g	An air mass coming from a warm ocean will be cold and dry.	☐	☐
h	Warm air always moves from a warmer place to a colder one.	☐	☐
i	The UK is closer to the equator than to the north pole.	☐	☐

2 The diagram below right shows what happens when a warm air mass arrives. The text below explains what happens – but it is in the wrong order. Put it in the right order by writing numbers 1–4 next to it.

☐ The rising air cools. The water vapour condenses to form a sloping bank of cloud.

☐ Warm air is lighter. So it slides up over the cold air.

☐ It starts to rain. It may rain for hours.

☐ As it rises, the pressure falls. So the weather gets a bit windy.

3 Draw the weather symbol for;

a A warm front

b A cold front

Finish the sentences.

A warm front means ______________________________

A cold front means ______________________________

5.7 A winter of storms

This is about storms that can badly affect the UK.

pages 80-81

1 You work on a newspaper and have been asked to write about how storms affect the UK.
Fill in the spaces below and give your story a catchy headline at the top.

The storm was caused…

People and places were affected in many different ways.

5.8 From weather to climate

pages 82-83

This is about climate and climate graphs.

1 Complete the following statements.

Climate is … ____

Climate is worked out by … ____

____

A climate graph shows … ____

2 The map shows the four climate regions for the UK. Below it is a climate graph for one place in each region.

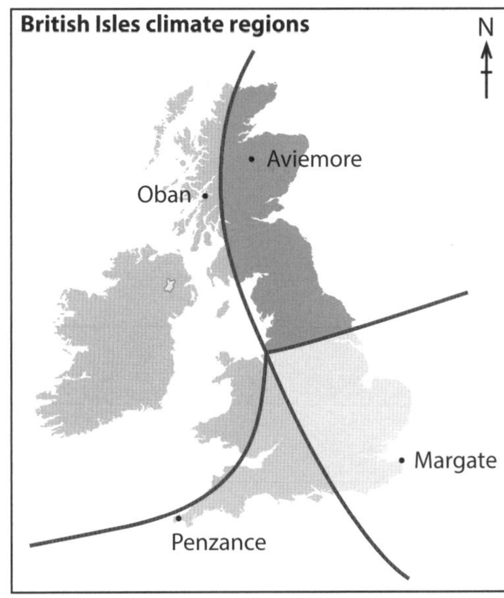

a Complete the table using information from the graphs.

	Oban	Aviemore	Penzance	Margate
Jan temp °C				
July temp °C				
Jan rainfall mm				
July rainfall mm				
Total rainfall				

b Choose two of the locations from the map. Say which ones you have chosen and describe what the weather will be like in winter and summer in those two places. Use information from the table above and the climate graphs to help you.

____

____

____

____

____

____

____

____

____

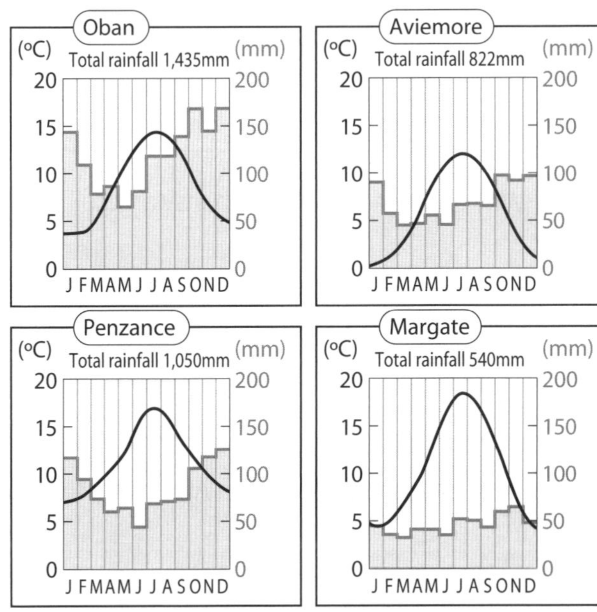

Note Aviemore is 230 m above sea level. All the other locations lie at sea level.

5.9 The factors that influence climate

pages 84-85

This is about why climate is different in different places.

1 Draw a line to match each factor affecting climate with the correct effect below.

Factors	**Effects**
Latitude	In the UK, the North Atlantic drift warms the west coast in winter.
Distance from the coast	The further you go from the equator the cooler it gets.
Prevailing wind direction	A sea breeze keeps the coast cool in summer and warm in winter.
Ocean currents	In the UK, it's from the south west and brings rain.
Height above sea level/altitude	The higher you are above sea level the cooler it is.

2 Look at the map and answer the questions.

a Why is Margate always warmer than Aviemore?

____

____

____

b Why will Leicester be warmer than Margate in summer, but cooler in winter?

____

____

____

c Why is Penzance wetter than Margate?

____

____

____

d Why is Oban warmer than Aviemore in winter?

____

____

____

5.10 Climates around the world

This is about climate in different parts of the world.

geog.2

pages 86-87

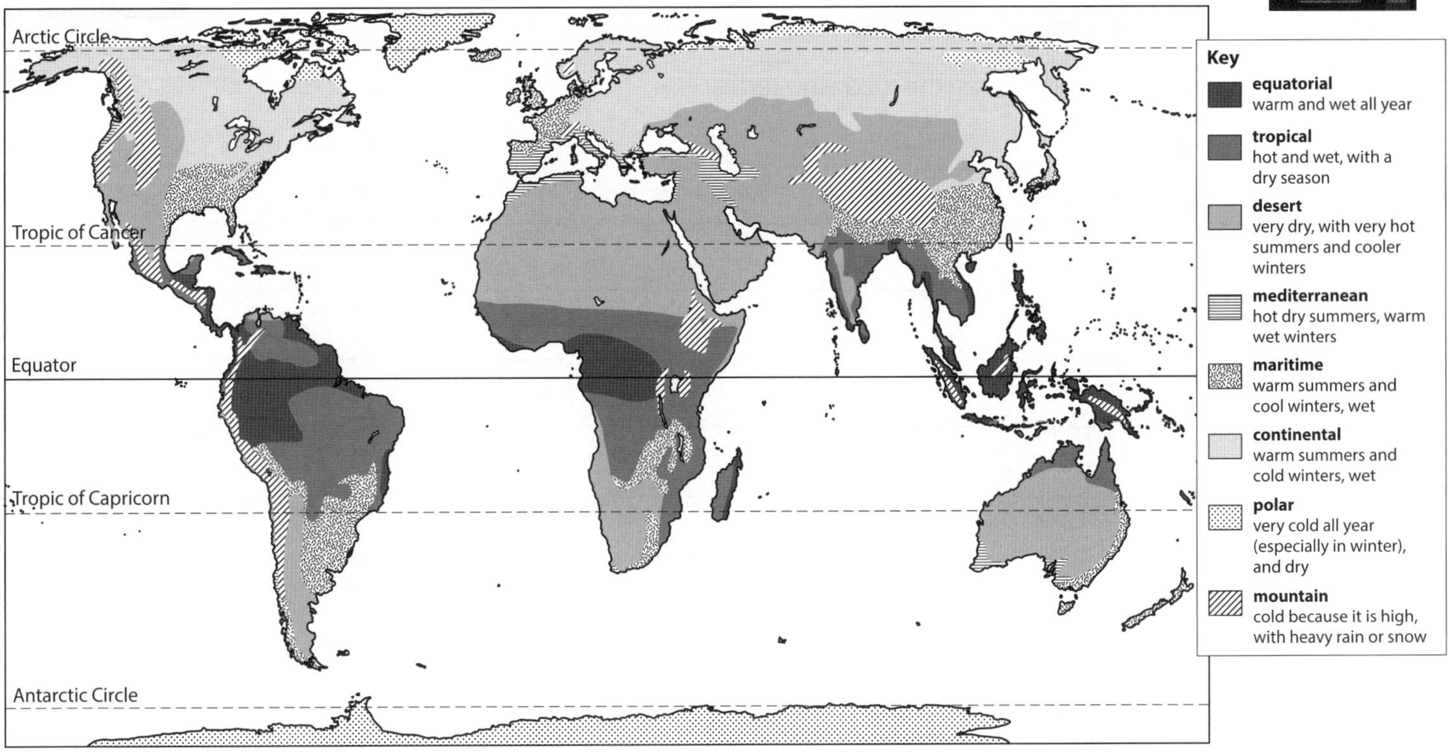

1 The map shows how the climate varies across the globe.
Choose one of the climates where you would like to go on holiday to. Explain why.

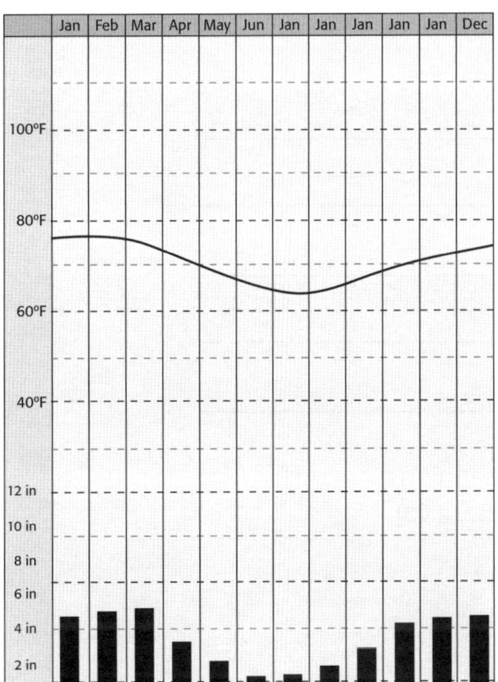

Name of climate ______________________

____

____

2 Look at this climate graph for Durban in South Africa.Compare the climate of Durban with that of London. Use the graph on page 83 of the student book to help you and use numbers/figures from the graphs to help your answer.

Temperature ______________________

____

____

Rainfall ______________________

____

____

6 Our warming planet

pages 88-89

1 What do you know about our warming planet?

Write down what you understand by the following terms:

Global warming

Climate change

Emissions

2 At the end of this topic, come back and see if you were right about these things
If you were, draw a ☺ next to what you have written - if you haven't, draw a ☹!

6.1 Earth's temperature through the ages

pages 90-91

Here you will learn more about three periods in our history when the climate was different from today.

Roman Britain was warmer that it is today. Find out how the warm climate helped the Romans to settle Britain, as well as growing grapes.

Find out more about how the Vikings settled Greenland, including the story of how it got its name!

Find out more about our 'Little Ice Age, including the 'Frost Fairs' that took place on the River Thames.

6.2 Global warming

This is about the reasons behind global warming.

pages 92-93

'The data proves it's mostly our fault'

'We are damaging our planet for the future'

'Some people say it's our fault, others say it is a natural event. I'm confused.

'I need my car. How am I supposed to work without it?'

1 Look at what the people are saying above. Give one reason why they have that point of view.

Scientist ______________________________

____

Environmentalist ______________________________

____

Pupil ______________________________

____

Driver ______________________________

____

2 Which one of the above do you agree with? Circle your choice and explain why.

Scientist Environmentalist Pupil Driver

____

____

____

____

6.3 Climate change

This is about how our warming planet may affect us all.

geog.2 pages 94-95

1 Read what is written in the boxes around the map. Draw arrows from each of the boxes to where they may happen on the map. One has been done for you.

- More heat waves in places like Europe
- Tourist areas might get too hot (e.g. Jamaica in the Caribbean)
- Animals and plants may die out (e.g. polar bear)

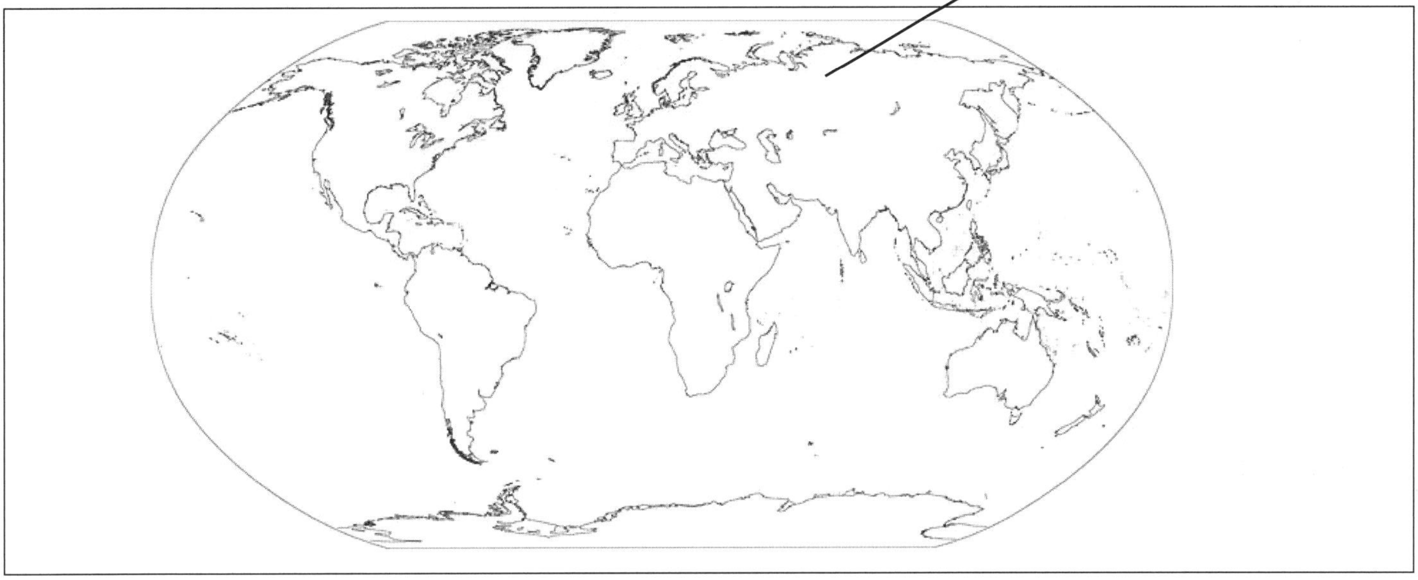

- More violent storms and floods (e.g. Central America)
- Rising seas will drown low-lying places like Bangladesh
- More diseases will spread as places warm up (e.g. cholera in Africa)
- Ice in the Polar regions will melt
- More refugees because of floods, or drought and famine (e.g. Sudan)
- Some places may grow new crops (e.g. Canada)

2 Look at the effects of global warming in the boxes. Are any of them good for us?

____

____

Why?

____

____

6.4 It's happening already!

This will make you think about the impact of global warming on human populations

geog.2 pages 96-97

See the drawings below which tell you about the impact of global warming on two very different animals.

Humans are being affected in the same way.

1 Write about what you think will happen to human populations around the world as global warming increases.

____

____

____

____

2 What is likely to happen as a result of this movement of humans?

____

____

____

____

3 Research the impact of global warming on one particular group of people and write about what has happened to them.

____

____

____

____

6.5 Who will suffer most?

This is about the things we do that produce carbon dioxide.

pages 98-99

'Worldmapper' maps are specially drawn maps. They don't show the actual shape and size of each country. They show countries in different sizes depending on what is being measured. Look at the maps below and spot how different the world looks.

This is a map of where toys are from. Toys are made in many parts of the world. Many toys are plastic which is made from oil. The map below shows that China and Hong Kong (on the right) is by far the largest country on the map. This means that it exports, or sells, more toys than any other country.

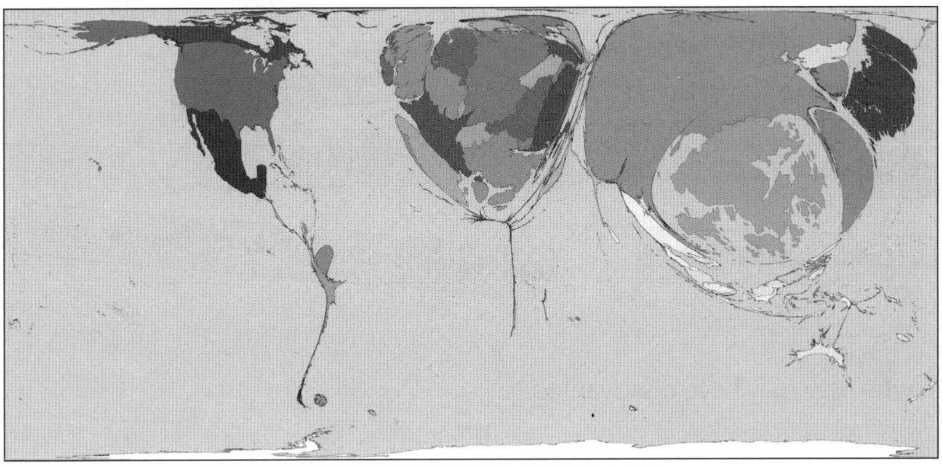

1 Why do you think that China is producing more and more carbon dioxide? Think about the effects of burning oil.

____

____

The map below shows toy imports (the countries that buy the toys). The USA is now the largest country.

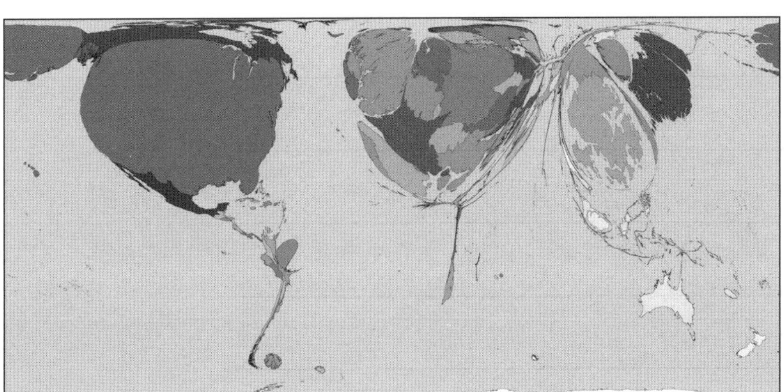

2 This is a very different map. Who should be blamed for increasing oil use – and why?

____

____

6.6 So what can we do?

This is about stopping or slowing down global warming.

pages 100-101

These actions could help to stop global warming.

1 Give out free bikes to everyone

2 Breed plants that will gobble up carbon dioxide

3 Put big taxes on air travel

4 Build more windfarms, for electricity

5 Don't turn on the heating. Just put on warm clothes

6 Turn off all the town and city lights at night

7 Shut down all power stations that use oil, coal or gas

8 Allow homes to have electricity for only 6 hours a day

9 Find a way to bury carbon dioxide under the ocean

10 Pass a law that women can only have one child each

11 Shoot millions of small mirrors into space, to reflect some sunlight away

12 Ban international events like the Olympic games

1 Choose **two** of these actions and explain why they may have disadvantages.

Number [ ] ______________________________

____

Number [ ] ______________________________

____

2 Choose one of the actions that you think is the best. Write a letter to the Prime Minister explaining your view.

____

____

____

____

____

____

____

7 Asia

geog.2 pages 102-103

1 Test yourself. Without looking anywhere else, draw an outline of Asia in the box below. Then draw in the borders of all the countries you can think of. Include the names of cities, mountains, rivers, lakes and deserts.

2 Write down all you know about three of the places you have put on the map.

Place 1 ____

____

Place 2 ____

____

Place 3 ____

____

3 At the end of this topic, come back and see if you've been correct about these places. Draw a ☺ next to each place you got more or less right. If you were wrong draw a ☹ next to the place!

7.1 What and where is Asia?

This is about locating the continent of Asia on the world map.

geog.2 pages 104-105

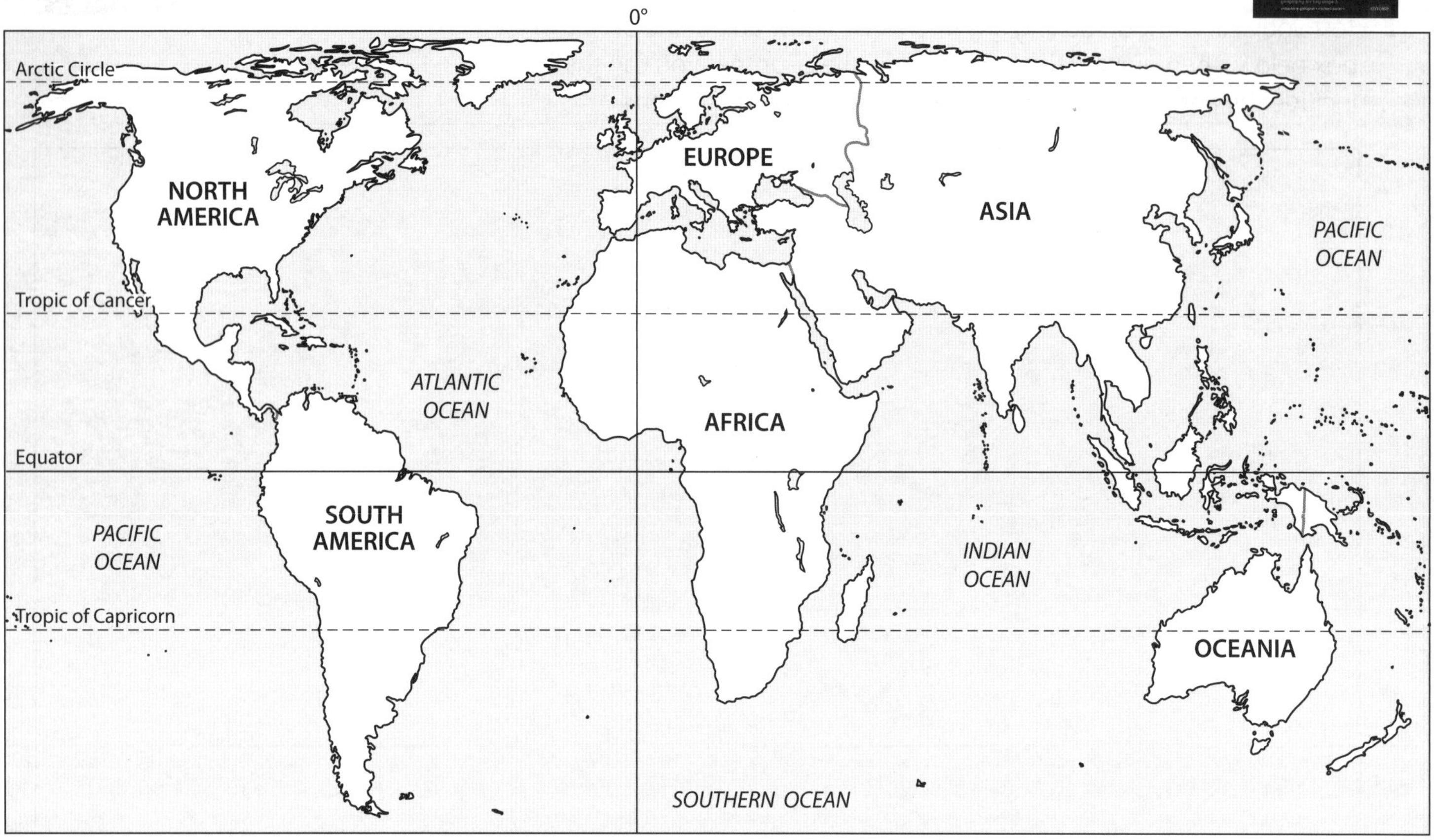

1 Colour in all the land in Asia that lies between the Tropic of Cancer and the Tropic of Capricorn. This area is known as the 'tropics' and is the hottest part of the world.

2 Using a second colour, colour in all the land in Asia that lies north of the Arctic Circle. This area is known as the Arctic. It is one of the world's two polar regions. They are the coldest parts of the world.

a Where does Asia have most land – inside the tropics or inside the Arctic Circle?

____

b Asia stretches from the tropics to the Arctic. What other continent stretches from the tropics to the Arctic?

____

c Name the island that lies half in Asia, half in Oceania.

____

3 Using a third colour fill in all the land area of Asia that lies outside the tropics and outside the Arctic. What proportion of Asia lies neither within the tropics nor within the Arctic? Circle the correct answer.

A About 65% B About 80% C About 50%

4 The map also shows the equator. Shade in the parts of Asia that lie south of the equator.

7.2 Asia's countries and regions

This will help you understand Asia's size and the variety of its countries and regions.

pages 106-107

1 Write down the names of the capital cities of the following countries

a China ______ **b** Iran ______ **c** Sri Lanka ______

d Iraq ______ **e** Cambodia ______ **f** Mongolia ______

g Saudi Arabia ______ **h** Kazakhstan ______ **i** Pakistan ______

2 Where are the Urals? You can find the Ural Mountains which form the border between Europe and Asia on page 112 of the Student's Book. Draw a line to show them on the map above.

3 Once you have drawn in the Urals on the map, guess which is the larger, China or Asian Russia?

______

4 Find the UK on the map. What is the quickest way to get to the UK by sea from Japan? Why is this not possible for most of the year?

______

______

______

7.3 A little history

This will help you understand what we owe to Chinese and Indian civilisations.

pages 108-109

1 India is the home of Buddhism. The first emperor to unite India was Ashoka who ruled from 269 to 232 BC. He was converted to Buddhism. Find out more about Ashoka. Why did he convert to Buddhism? Why is he considered to be one of India's greatest rulers?

2 Many important discoveries have been made in China. They include paper (about AD 100), the magnetic compass (about AD 100|) and gunpowder (about AD 800).

Write about how important these discoveries were to us.

a Paper

b Gunpowder

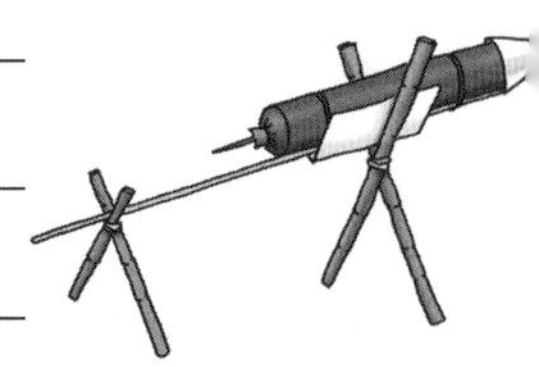

The Chinese used rockets and cannon 600 years before we did.

c The magnetic compass

What's Asia like?

This will help to identify Asia's largest cities and put them into rank order.

geog.2
pages 110-111

Asia, home of the megacity?

Only 42% of the Asia's population lives in urban areas; however, it has the second fastest urban population growth rate, of any continent.
Many claims are made for the growth of Asia's 'megacities'. The figures below for the 20 largest cities in Asia from the United Nations are for the wider built up areas of cities rather than just the actual city boundary.

1 Place these cities into rank order and identify which country they lie in.

City	Population (millions)	Country	Rank Order
Bangalore	8.45		
Bangkok	8.28		
Beijing	12.39		
Chongqing	9.40		
Delhi	22.16		
Dhaka	14.65		
Guangzhou	8.88		
Istanbul	10.52		
Jakarta	9.21		
Karachi	13.12		
Kolkata	15.55		
Manila	11.63		
Moscow	10.55		
Mumbai	20.04		
Osaka-Kobe	11.34		
Seoul	9.77		
Shanghai	16.58		
Shenzhen	9.01		
Tianjin,	9.34		
Tokyo	36.67		

2 It is very difficult to find agreement about the size of the world's largest cities. Can you think of reasons why estimates vary?

7.5 Asia's physical features

Here we look at the relationship between Asia's physical features and its countries.

pages 112-113

1 Compare the map on page 112 of the student book with the political map on page 106 and answer the following questions;

a Which countries are the Himalayas in?

___

b In which countries does the Gobi Desert lie?

___

c In which country is Lake Baykal?

___

d In which country are the Zagros Mountains?

___

e Name 5 rivers that rise on the Plateau of Tibet.

___

___

2 On the map:

a circle the three groups of islands that are part of India..

b circle the highest and lowest points in Asia.
What is the difference in height between them? ___

c Circle the three islands named on the map that are part of the Philippines.

3 Research and find out what is unusual about the Aral Sea.

___

___

___

___

___

___

___

7.6 Asia's population

Here we look at the relationship between Asia's population and its physical features.

pages 114-115

Compare the map of Asia's population distribution on page 114 of the student book with the map of Asia's physical features on page 112 of the student book.

1 In many parts of Asia, but especially in Siberia, the low level density population distribution looks 'stripey'. Can you explain the reason for this?

____

____

2 In the far west of China, near the Mongolian and Kazakhstan borders, there is a city of nearly three million people in an otherwise sparsely populated area. Identify this city and write about its history and its importance today.

____

____

____

____

3 Look up Indonesia on the political and physical maps of Asia on pages 106 and 112 of the student book.

a What do you notice about the population density of Java compared with the other islands of Indonesia?

____

b Can you explain this difference in population density?

____

____

4 The overall population density of Mongolia is 2 people per square kilometre, while the overall population density of China is 139 people per square kilometre. Explain why figures like this can be misleading with reference to the map on page 114 of the student book.

____

____

7.7 Asia's biomes

This is about telling what biome a place is in from its weather statistics.

pages 116-117

The letters on the map represent five cities;

Shanghai Lhasa Verkhoyansk Singapore Aden

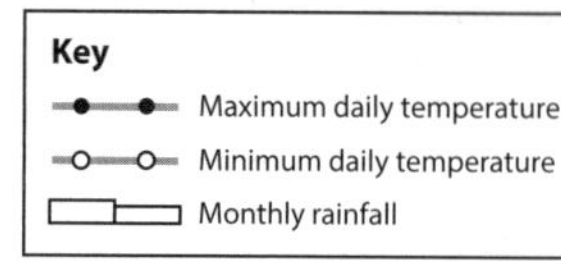

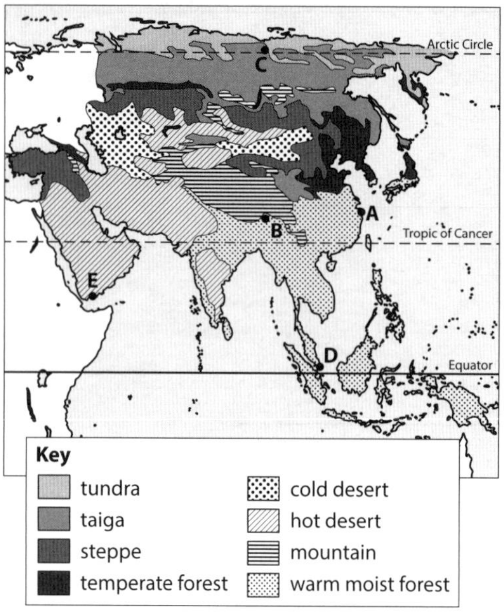

Here are the climate charts for these places. Match each place to a chart and write down which biome it represents (tundra, mountain, temperate forest, hot desert, tropical/sub-tropical) Also write down the reasons you matched that place to its biome.

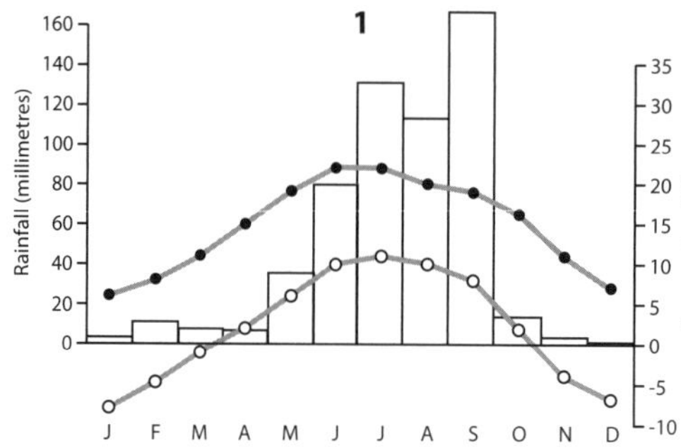

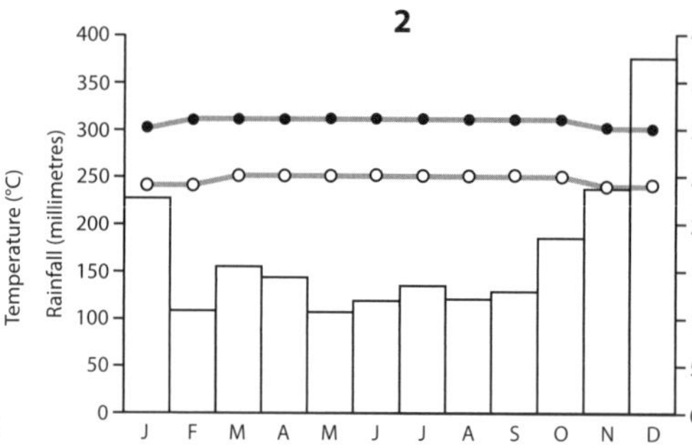

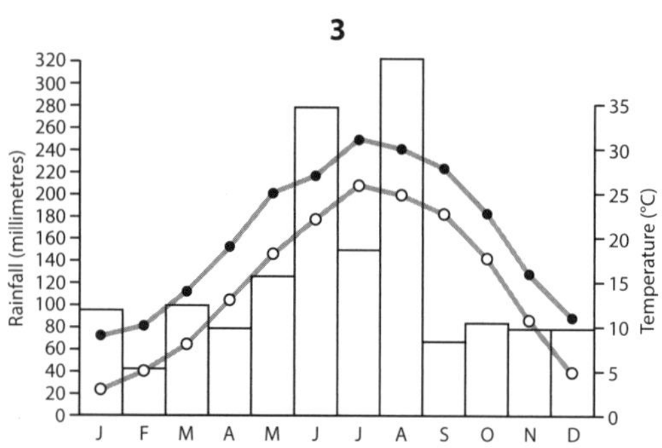

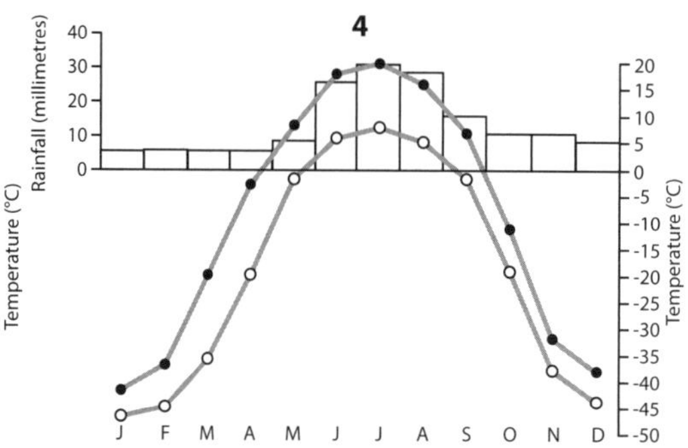

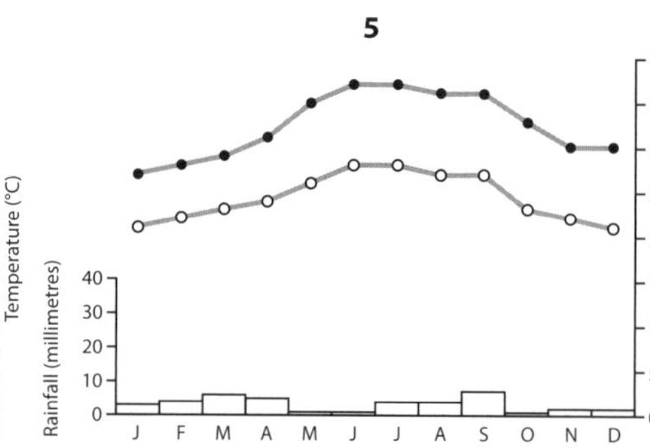

Place A (elevation 140m) Chart number ________ Name ____________ Biome ____________

Reasons ____

Place B (elevation 3600m) Chart number ________ Name ____________ Biome ____________

Reasons ____

Place C (elevation sea level) Chart number ________ Name ____________ Biome ____________

Reasons ____

Place D (elevation sea level) Chart number ________ Name ____________ Biome ____________

Reasons ____

Place E (elevation sea level) Chart number ________ Name ____________ Biome ____________

Reasons ____

8 Southwest China

geog.2 pages 118-119

Look carefully at the photographs on page 118 in the pupil book. Imagine you are a web news producer and have been given the images to use in a short video piece for a web site about Southwest China. You have two tasks:

1. Decide in which order you want to present the images. Write the number from 1 to 6 in the tick box top left of each text box.

2. Write a brief commentary to go with each photo. Remember, the website is aiming to introduce Southwest China to people who have not been there!

8.1 China: an overview

What is blue, a quarter of a mile long and taller than London's Olympic stadium?

pages 120-121

1 China is the world's top exporter of goods. Many of the things you buy will have travelled from China on huge container ships like the one described and shown. They can carry 15 000 containers! Find FIVE things that you or your family own that were made in China. Inside the drawing of a container below, sketch and label your five items.

2 Write four sentences to explain why China is so important to your daily life. Remember to include reasons for your answer.

8.2 The rise of China

This is about some of the important changes that have happened in China.

pages 122-123

1 Some of the major changes that have affected China are shown below. Circle whether the statements are true or false.

Changes since 1979	True or False?
Farmers can now farm land for themselves, and sell the extra food they produce	True False
Foreign companies are not allowed to set up in China	True False
All families have to have at least one child	True False
Farmers are allowed to sell the extra food they produce	True False
China trades more with the rest of the world	True False
Forty years ago few Chinese people lived in poverty	True False
The Chinese people were free to make their own choices before the changes	True False

2 The decisions taken by the Chinese government have led to some successful changes.

In 1981, 85% of Chinese lived in poverty. Today the figure is about 7%.

China is now the world's top exporter of manufactured goods.

China now has the second largest economy in the world, after the USA.

The one-child policy has prevented around 400 million births.

Millions of people have moved from rural areas to work in the factories.

The rate of urbanisation in China is the fastest the world has ever seen.

China now has many new factories, making goods for export.

Most new factories are in cities and towns in the east, along and near the coast.

Colour in the one change that you think is most significant to China and its people. Give reasons for your choice in the space below.

8.3 China's Southwest region

This is where you will learn more about the Southwest region of China.

pages 124-125

	Population (millions)	Population density (people per km²)	% of population that is urban	GDP per person PPP (dollars)
Tibet	3	2.2	15	6138
Sichuan	81	170	33	7642
Chongqing	30	350	49	10 077
Guizhou	35	200	35	3100
Yunnan	46	120	33	4160
UK	64	263	80	37 000

1 Study the data about Southwest China.

a How many times larger is the population of Chongqing than Tibet? __________

b In which area do almost half the people live in towns and cities? __________

c Which part of Southwest China has a GDP that is $4 542 less than Sichuan? __________

d What percentage of Tibet's population lives in the countryside? __________

2 On the map label the five smaller areas of Southwest China – Tibet, Sichuan, Chongqing, Guizhou and Yunnan.

3 In the table below, choose and write down three interesting facts about each of the five areas.

Tibet	• • •
Sichuan	• • •
Chongqing	• • •
Guizhou	• • •
Yunnan	• • •

4 Choose the one area which you would like to visit most, and give reasons for your answer.

I would most like to visit __________

8.4 Chongqing

Hold onto your seats – this area is growing fast!

pages 126-127

1 Fill in the gaps in the following passage using words from the box below.

Chongqing is controlled from ____________. It is a little ____________ than Scotland and most of it is ____________. Chongqing city lies at the confluence of two rivers; this means where the rivers ____________. Chongqing is an inland port. This means that large ____________ can travel from the port of ____________, 2380 km away. There are many ____________ industries, making products such as cars, textiles and computers. Farmers in the rural areas keep pigs, and grow rice and ____________.

bigger	rural	ships	oranges
meet	Shanghai	manufacturing	Beijing

2 Chongqing city is growing fast and many people are moving there. In the speech bubbles below write what these people would think about the developments in the city. Remember to give reasons for your answers!

8.5 Life in Chongqing

This is about the lives of some of the people who live and work in Chongqing.

geog.2 pages 128-129

The Happy Planet Index (HPI) is a global measure of sustainable well-being. The HPI measures what matters: the extent to which countries deliver long, happy, sustainable lives for the people that live in them. The Index uses global data on life expectancy, experienced well-being and Ecological Footprint to calculate this.

1 China has a Happy Planet Index of 44.7 and is ranked at number 60 out of 151 countries. How happy do you think Liu Jian, Wang Hua, Wu Shan and He Chan feel? Circle the number for each of them on the scale below and give reasons to explain your choice.

Happiness Scale

Liu Jian, a bang-bang man

Very Unhappy ⊢ - - - - - - - - - - - - - - - - ⊣ Very Happy

0 1 2 3 4 5

Reason for decision ______________________________

____

____

Wang Hua, factory worker

Very Unhappy ⊢ - - - - - - - - - - - - - - - - ⊣ Very Happy

0 1 2 3 4 5

Reason for decision ______________________________

____

____

Wu Shan, restaurant owner

Very Unhappy ⊢ - - - - - - - - - - - - - - - - ⊣ Very Happy

0 1 2 3 4 5

Reason for decision ______________________________

____

____

He Chan, a left behind

Very Unhappy ⊢ - - - - - - - - - - - - - - - - ⊣ Very Happy

0 1 2 3 4 5

Reason for decision ______________________________

____

____

8.6 Tops for biodiversity!

Panda-monium - this is all about China's panda population.

pages 130-131

1 Read these statements about China's and its pandas.

A

"Sichuan's panda sanctuaries are home to around a third of the world's population of pandas."

B

"Seven nature reserves and nine parks lie next to the Qionglai and Jiajin mountains. The sanctuaries are also home to red pandas, snow and cloud leopards."

C

"Pandas are the poster animals for the zoo industry. They receive millions of pounds worth of support. I think this money would be better spent preserving their habitat instead so that they can stay in the wild."

D

"Bamboo is the main food of pandas. It is estimated that half of the world bamboo forests have disappeared since 1974."

E

"In May 2013 the world's first panda-themed hotel opened for business in Sichuan."

F

"Most captive-breeding programs eventually want to reintroduce the animals back into China's bamboo forests – but can they survive in the forests?"

G

"In Ya'an, about an hour and a half away from the city of Chengdu, tourism chiefs aim to create a giant panda capital."

H

"Possibly as few as 1,600 giant pandas remain in the wild, and more than 300 live in captivity around the globe"

2 Using the information above, write a 70 word speech explaining your view about pandas and their survival.

Tip: Be as persuasive as you can!

3 Suggest one idea that you think will have most chance of helping pandas to survive. Give reasons for your answer.

8.7 Tibet

Here you will find out more about Tibet, China's 'Roof of the World'.

pages 132-133

1 This paragraph describes Tibet. Choose words from the box to fill in the gaps.

Tibet is over ten times ____________ than the UK and over 4.5 km ____________ on average. At the ____________ edge of the plateau, the Himalayas begin. Tibet is cold, and the winds can be ____________ . Much of the country is Tundra, with permanently frozen soil and no ____________ . Tibet is ____________ for nine months of the year, but has thousands of ____________ and lakes.

high dry trees vicious wet glaciers southern people bigger reservoirs

2 Explain why Tibet is often called the 'Roof of the World'.

____

____

____

3 An extreme environment has harsh and challenging conditions – because of its location, its ecosystem, climate or landscape. Humans and animals often need to adapt in order to survive in it. To what extent do you think Tibet is an extreme environment? Give reasons for your answer.

Tip: Use facts and figures from the pupil book pages to help you decide! **!**

____

____

____

____

____

____

4 'Earth bit hiss' is an anagram for three words that could be used to describe Tibet.

Can you decode the anagram? ____________________

Do you agree? Give reasons for your answer.

____

____

____

8.8 All change in Tibet

This is about some of the important changes happening in Tibet.

pages 134-135

1 Using your own words annotate the photograph below to explain why China is making some of the changes in Tibet.

> Tip: Think of the reasons, and what benefits the changes may bring to Tibet. **!**

Transport

Mining

Water

Land

2 Imagine you are one of the local people shown in the photograph. What would you think about the changes? Choose the one that you think would benefit you the most. Explain your answer.

I think that the changes in Tibet will ______________________________

____

____

The one change that would most benefit me is ______________________________

____

____

8.9 The rivers and dams

This is all about China's big plans for building dams.

pages 136-137

1 This wordsearch is all about China and its plans to capture its water. Find the words shown on the right.

m	m	j	p	w	u	f	e	z	r	b	z	w	p	g
s	e	w	j	a	r	l	l	o	t	q	r	t	l	r
r	f	l	y	r	e	v	e	y	s	m	s	o	q	q
e	m	q	t	m	s	u	c	a	m	t	b	h	c	b
i	i	v	o	i	g	z	t	e	a	a	y	j	a	e
c	n	v	w	n	n	n	r	t	l	m	m	l	a	n
a	f	w	l	g	j	g	i	n	c	j	b	r	a	s
l	a	p	o	l	w	b	c	q	s	c	t	j	c	e
g	h	r	h	r	a	t	i	c	g	h	c	n	q	e
a	z	h	p	h	d	t	t	h	q	n	h	b	j	r
p	l	a	t	e	a	u	y	u	r	m	o	p	m	t
p	f	y	a	d	g	h	a	z	o	l	p	h	t	p
n	g	g	q	z	i	k	y	k	n	j	e	u	c	i
e	z	u	d	j	e	n	o	i	t	u	l	l	o	p
w	b	z	j	s	r	e	t	a	w	x	g	n	m	h

chongqing
drown
earthquakes
electricity
glaciers
global
habitats
melting
plateau
pollution
trees
warming
water

2 In the space below, write a paragraph about China and its dams. You must use all of the words that you found in the wordsearch!